117 DAYS

An Account of Confinement and Interrogation under
the South African Ninety-Day Detention Law

RUTH FIRST

BLOOMSBURY

First published 1965
This edition published 1988

Copyright © 1965 by the Estate of Ruth First
Introduction to this edition © 1988 by Joe Slovo

Bloomsbury Publishing Ltd, 2 Soho Square, London W1V 5DE

British Library Cataloguing in Publication Data

First, Ruth, *1925-1982*
117 days.
1. South Africa.   Political prisoners.
Prison life, 1964- Personal observations
I. Title
365′.45′0924

ISBN 0-7475-0233-1

Printed in Great Britain by Clays,
Bungay, Suffolk

CONTENTS

INTRODUCTION TO NEW EDITION *

I last saw Ruth alive on the day it happened at about 3.30 in the afternoon. I was talking with our close friend, Harold Wolpe, when she rushed into the lounge through the front door and reached out for the bottle of wine which she had forgotten to take with her earlier. With an embarrassed smile and a clipped, 'I'm a real scatter-brain, see you later,' she was gone. The wine, never uncorked, was intended for a celebratory toast in her office with a few colleagues departing from a conference she had helped organize.

At about 4.30 the telephone rang. The broken voice of her colleague, Marc Wuyts, is still audible in my mind. 'Joe, something terrible has happened. There's been an explosion and Ruth is just lying there . . . ' She had died instantly. When I arrived, the overwhelming urge to remember her in life paralysed me at the entrance to her devastated office. She lay hidden by the remnants of her desk; only her feet were visible, clad in one of her stylish beige-coloured pairs of shoes.

For Ruth it had been an exhilarating and frenetic week; a high-point of her position as Director of Research of the Centre for African Studies at the Eduardo Mondlane University in Maputo, in recently independent Mozambique. Scholars had assembled from every part of Southern Africa, with a sprinkling from beyond, to participate in what turned out to be a highly successful UNESCO-supported workshop. And the obvious focus was the race tyranny not more than forty miles away in apartheid South Africa.

Ruth had brought to her post at the Centre a rare combination of gifts: a razor-sharp intellect, a flow of language which enabled her to communicate complex ideas simply, a deft organizational talent, an ethic of meticulous preparation, and an approach to teaching which firmly situated the student in society. She had already spent a good part of her adult life in non-academic pursuits, as social worker, journalist, author, public campaigner and underground activist. She had had many books published and was very highly regarded among academics. And, through it all, and through the traumas of police harassment and imprisonment, she carved out the time and the energy to be a caring mother to our daughters Shawn, Gillian and Robyn, and the space for our thirty-three years of warm, albeit spirited, companionship in marriage.

*This introduction was written for the new edition of *117 Days* by Ruth First's husband, Joe Slovo, who now lives in exile in Zambia, the only white member of the executive committee of the African National Congress.

4

Introduction

She projected great strength, businesslike confidence and a degree of arrogance; a façade, recognized by those who knew her well, designed to cover her extreme vulnerability and a warmth and passion she found it hard to display. She never really conquered a touching uncertainty about her talents; a feeling which was not appeased by her enviable record of personal achievement. All this made her react defensively to criticism and she felt exposed even by so trivial a public lapse as forgetting to take the bottle of wine.

From Swaziland in May 1960, where she had gone with the children to evade the post-Sharpeville Emergency detentions, she had written to me in the prison where I was being held:

> My introspection gets more and more involved as I go in for my favourite pastime of undermining me and my character and seeing my faults ... Pity I never had any talent for philosophy. Then my conflicts wouldn't have to be on a personal plane ... Trouble really is I would like to prove to myself I can produce something worthwhile ... But I'm too directionless and I know at heart that if direction, application and talent aren't there, it's all my own undoing and no one can overcome that. But, as you say, I'll get over this and be absorbed tomorrow in something or other. It's a form of masochism I suffer from; one of my afflictions, like heavy eyebrows and a mole on my nose.

I know that it was especially hard for Ruth to write *117 Days*; the first book of its genre to appear in the phase after the Rivonia trial at which Nelson Mandela and other underground leaders were jailed for life. Once committed to the task, she was faced with having to bare quite a few of her 'moles', both imagined and real. But she was moved to go ahead in the hope that the narrative would help focus world attention on the plight of the growing number of victims of the regime's physical and mental torture-machine. Indeed, the book was later made into a TV film by the BBC and, more recently, was a major inspiration for my daughter Shawn's film script for *A World Apart*.

Ruth was among the first batch of detainees on whom the Special Branch (straight from refresher courses in Western police academies) began to practise their newly acquired skills of mental torture. It was a technique based on a diabolically simple principle: assault the prisoner's only companion in an isolation cell – the mind. For the early victims of this type of torture it was all the more frightening because they did not know what awaited them and were, therefore, poorly prepared to cope with it.

In addition, in the case of Ruth, the Security Branch had someone at their mercy whose involvements in the political underground had been central and extensive. There was little that she did not know about the Rivonia headquarters and its national network of underground structures. It was with this terrible burden that she stood up to her inquisitors. When she began to fear that she might be approaching cracking-point – an abortive attempt at an innocuous statement that both humiliated her and made her suspect a loss of control and judgement – she tried to kill herself.

> I was persecuted by the dishonour of having made . . . even the start
> of a statement . . . I was in a state of collapse . . . for the gnawing
> ugly fear that they could destroy me among the people whose
> understanding and succour I most needed, and that once they had
> done that I would have nothing left to live for . . . There was only
> one way out . . .

After her release, when we all knew that (in the last prophetic words of her book) 'it was not the end, that they would come again', she responded to my appeals, that she and the children should move quickly to join me in London, by writing, 'I don't want to be indecently hasty for reasons you will understand. Rushing ahead oblivious to a local consideration will be sad and misunderstood.' I understood the reasons; the 'local consideration' was the tottering underground which 'bitter-enders' like Bram Fischer were courageously battling to keep alive. I still blush at the fact that it was she, who had just been through so much, who had had to remind me.

In the event, they came again – nineteen years later – on 17th August 1982, in the form of a letter-bomb which exploded. At first glance, Ruth did not appear to be a priority target. She was not associated with the planning or implementation of the type of resistance activity the authorities feared most – armed actions. She was no longer the full-time liberation publicist of her journalistic days. She was a veteran South African Communist Party member but was not, at the time, serving on any of its leading bodies; in fact she was out on a limb because of her outspoken aversion to the ghastly crimes of Stalin and the tragic consequences they brought for the kind of socialism in which she so passionately believed. Why then was she chosen? Her selection as a target was neither capricious nor accidental; it served a special purpose which, with the passage of time, could be identified more clearly.

Pretoria sensed that it had done enough to create a mood of desperation within the young Southern African states still trying to find their feet in the post-independence era. Direct military attacks, economic destabilization and the unleashing of bandit armies had, indeed, inflicted severe wounds. And the victims, with so few resources to meet the onslaught, were beginning to feel abandoned. The Reagans of the world were 'constructively' engaged on the side of this thuggery and the Thatchers sabotaged every international attempt to take effective measures against it; arousing a suspicion that the protection of 'kith and kin' overshadowed their concern for 'human rights' and their much-vaunted repudiation of state terrorism. And the rest of the world seemed unready or unable to provide the means, economic and military, with which the blows could be parried or sustained.

In the period immediately preceding Ruth's murder, these considerations prompted Botha's strategic think-tank to consider fresh diplomatic manoeuvres. The stick, they speculated, appeared to have made an impression. Those against whom it had been wielded must surely have absorbed the lesson that the alternatives before them were – to parody Botha's phrase – either to adapt to Pretoria's will or to continue dying. In order finally to spike the guns of the ANC-led liberation alliance, a probe seemed plausible in the direction of 'mutual security agreements'. Beginning with Swaziland, which was, for some years, too ashamed publicly to acknowledge its treaty with Pretoria, the racist regime set its sights on the bigger prize, Mozambique.

For those charged with preparing the ground for these new tactical options, the elimination of Ruth must have figured as relevant to the equation. They knew that the whole thrust of her teaching tended to counter some creeping illusions and wishful thinking about Botha; that he might be ready to retreat from the essence of apartheid towards a policy of true reform, and that he could perhaps be trusted to honour the principles of co-existence and good-neighbourliness. And Ruth was not working in an ivory tower; the students at the Centre were cadres from the Party and the government, and the dynamism and vigour of the Centre were beginning to influence researchers and scholars from other institutions of learning in Southern Africa.

The growing impact of this work, both inside and outside Mozambique, must have been seen as directly relevant to the kind of response Pretoria could expect to offers of 'mutual security agreements'. The body of ideas which Ruth was promoting had no place in it for the expectation that a bargain with Pretoria of the Nkomati type could be anything other than a self-wounding exercise, as it indeed turned out to be. And so someone among these planners, programmed to consider options rather than human beings, ordered the parcel of death to be prepared and went off to have his dinner.

Ruth's assassination was part of a series of murders in every frontline state, each act having been designed by Pretoria to serve a specific policy purpose in countries which were tolerating an ANC presence within their borders. Joe Gqabi, for example, Ruth's one-time journalistic colleague on the *Guardian* and *New Age,* had been a victim a year earlier. He had recently finished a ten-year term of imprisonment on Robben Island and had become the ANC's chief representative in Zimbabwe. He had been gunned down outside his residence in Harare, an act which had wholly failed in its objective of terrorizing the fledgling state into having second thoughts about its support for South Africa's liberation forces. And years later the outstanding Mozambican President Samora Machel was himself killed when his aircraft was lured to destruction in South African hills by a false beacon.

In our orations we often try to mitigate the impact of such death-blows by emphasizing that the fallen will, through their very sacrifice, inspire an even greater advance of the cause for which they died. There is something in this long-term view, even though it can neither assuage personal anguish nor replenish political gaps. But there is a real sense in which our loss is not always the enemy's gain.

Imprisonment, torture (immeasurably grown in scale and sophistication since Ruth's detention), hangings, mass killings on the streets and the assassin's bomb and bullet have all demonstrably failed to cow the spirit of resistance to the race tyranny. Indeed, particularly in the last few years, it is over the very coffins of the slain that mass vows are taken, and thereafter honoured, to intensify the fight regardless of risks to life and limb.

Ruth's own funeral, as she was laid to rest alongside more than a dozen of her ANC comrades who had been assassinated by apartheid killer squads in Maputo, was an example of this. Hundreds of Mozambicans of all walks of life – government ministers, cleaners, soldiers, women and men, old and young, black and white – filed past the coffin while the ANC choir sang songs of our struggle for freedom.

117 Days is part of the inspiration which will inevitably lead to a society of justice and harmony in our land, and peace in the region. Of all Ruth's many books, it is by far the most intimate and personal. It is also a chronicle of signal bravery, all the more moving because Ruth showed no awareness of the courage with which she faced her tormentors.

March 1988   JOE SLOVO

Chapter One

THE CELL

For the first fifty-six days of my detention in solitary I changed from a mainly vertical to a mainly horizontal creature. A black iron bedstead became my world. It was too cold to sit, so I lay extended on the bed, trying to measure the hours, the days and the weeks, yet pretending to myself that I was not. The mattress was lumpy; the grey prison blankets were heavy as tarpaulins and smelt of mouldy potatoes. I learned to ignore the smell and to wriggle round the bumps in the mattress. Seen from the door the cell had been catacomb-like, claustrophobic. Concrete-cold. Without the naked electric bulb burning, a single yellow eye, in the centre of the ceiling, the cell would have been totally black; the bulb illuminated the grey dirt on the walls which were painted black two-thirds of the way up. The remaining third of the cell wall had been white once; the dust was a dirty film over the original surface. The window, high in the wall above the head of the bedstead, triple thick – barred, barred again and meshed – with sticky black soot on top of all three protective layers, was a closing, not an opening. Three paces from the door and I was already at the bed.

Left in that cell long enough, I feared to become one of those colourless insects that slither under a world of flat, grey stones, away from the sky and the sunlight, the grass and people. On the iron bedstead it was like being closed inside a matchbox. A tight fit, lying on my bed, I felt I should keep my arms straight at my sides in cramped, stretched-straight orderliness. Yet the bed was my privacy, my retreat, and could be my secret life. On the bed I felt in control of the cell. I did not need to survey it; I could ignore it, and concentrate on making myself comfortable. I would sleep, as long as I liked, without fear of interruption. I would think, without diversion. I would wait to see what happened, from the comfort of my bed.

Yet, not an hour after I was lodged in the cell, I found myself forced to do what storybook prisoners do: pace the length and breadth of the cell. Or tried, for there was not room enough to pace. The bed took up almost the entire length of the cell, and in the space remaining between it and the wall was a small protruding shelf. I could not walk round the cell, I could not even cross it. To measure its eight feet by six, I had to walk the length alongside the bed and the shelf, and then, holding my shoe in my hand, crawl under the bed to measure out the breadth. It seemed important to be accurate. Someone might ask me one day – when? – the size of my cell. The measuring done, I retreated to the bed. There were four main positions to take up: back, stomach, either side, and then variations, with legs stretched out or curled up. In a long night a shift in position had to be as adventurous as a walk. When my knees were curled up they lay level with a pin-scratched scrawl on the wall: '*I am here for murdering my baby. I'm 14 years.*' The wardresses told me they remembered that girl. They were vague about the authors of the other wall scribbles. '*Magda Loves Vincent for Ever*' appeared several times in devotedly persistent proclamation. Others conveyed the same sentiment but with lewd words and too-graphic illustrations, and in between the obscenities on the wall crawled the hearts and cupid's arrows. The women prisoners of the Sharpeville Emergency had left their mark in the '*Mayibuye i'Afrika*' [Let Africa Come Back] slogan still faintly visible. It was better not to look at the concrete walls, but even when I closed my eyes and sank deeper into the warmth of the bed, there were other reminders of the cell. The doors throughout the police station were heavy steel. They clanged as they were dragged to, and the reverberation hammered through my neck and shoulders, so that in my neck fibres I felt the echo down the passage, up the stairs, round the rest of the double-storey police station. The doors had no inside handles and these clanging doors without handles became, more than the barred window, more than the concrete cell walls, the humiliating reminder of incarceration, like the strait-jacket must be in his lucid moments to the violent inmate of an asylum.

The Cell

Six hours before my first view of the cell, I had come out of the main reading-room of the University library. The project that week was how to choose atlases in stocking a library, and in my hand was a sheaf of newly scribbled notes:

pre-1961 atlases almost as obsolete for practical usage as a 1920 road map – evaluate frequency and thoroughness of revision, examine speciality maps, e.g. distribution of resources and population – look for detail plus legibility – check consistency of scale in maps of different areas – indexes – explanations of technical and cartographic terms, etc. etc.

The librarianship course was an attempt to train for a new profession. My newest set of bans prohibited me from writing, from compiling any material for publication, from entering newspaper premises. Fifteen years of journalism had come to an end. I had worked for five publications and each had, in turn, been banned or driven out of existence by the Nationalist Government. There was no paper left in South Africa that would employ me, or could, without itself being an accomplice in the contravention of ministerial orders. So I had turned from interviewing ejected farm squatters, probing labour conditions and wages on gold mines, reporting strikes and political campaigns, to learning reference methods, cataloguing and classification of books, and I was finding the shelves poor substitutes for the people and the pace that had made up our newspaper life.

The two stiff men walked up.
'We are from the police.'
'Yes, I know.'
'Come with us, please. Colonel Klindt wants to see you.'
'Am I under arrest?'
'Yes.'
'What law?'
'Ninety Days,' they said.

Somehow, in the library as I packed up the reference books

on my table, I managed to slip out of my handbag and under a pile of lecture notes the note delivered to me from D. that morning. It had suggested a new meeting-place where we could talk. The place was 'clean' and unknown, D. had written. He would be there for a few days.

The two detectives ranged themselves on either side of me and we walked out of the University grounds. An Indian student looked at the escort and shouted: 'Is it all right?' I shook my head vigorously and he made a dash in the direction of a public telephone booth: there might be time to catch the late afternoon edition of the newspaper, and Ninety-Day detentions were 'news'.

The raid on our house lasted some hours. It was worse than the others, of previous years. Some had been mere formalities, incidents in the general police drive against 'agitators'; at the end of the 1956 raid, frightening and widespread as it was, there had been the prospect of a trial, albeit for treason. I tried to put firmly out of my mind the faces of the children as I was driven away. Shawn had fled into the garden so that I would not see her cry. Squashed on the front seat beside two burly detectives, with three others of rugby build on the back seat, I determined to show nothing of my apprehension at the prospect of solitary confinement, and yet I lashed myself for my carelessness. Under a pile of the *New Statesman* had been a single, forgotten copy of *Fighting Talk*, overlooked in the last clean-up in our house of banned publications. Possession of *Fighting Talk*, which I had edited for nine years, was punishable by imprisonment for a minimum of one year. Immediately, indefinite confinement for interrogation was what I had to grapple with. I was going into isolation to face a police probe, knowing that even if I held out and they could pin no charge on me, I had convicted myself by carelessness in not clearing my house of illegal literature: this thought became a dragging leaden guilt from then on.

The five police roughs joked in Afrikaans on the ride that led to Marshall Square Police Station. Only once did they direct themselves to me: 'We know lots,' one said. 'We know everything. You have only yourself to blame for this. We know. . . .'

It was about six in the afternoon when we reached the police station. The largest of my escorts carried my suitcase into the '*Europeans Only*' entrance. As he reached the charge office doorway he looked upwards 'Bye-bye, blue sky,' he said, and chuckled at his joke.

'Ninety days,' this Security Branch man told the policemen behind the counter.

'*Skud haar*' [Give her a good shake-up] the policeman in charge told the wardress.

When we came back from her office to the charge office, all three looked scornfully at my suitcase. 'You can't take this, or that, or this,' and the clothing was piled on the counter in a prohibited heap. A set of sheets was allowed in, a small pillow, a towel, a pair of pyjamas, and a dressing-gown. 'Not the belt!' the policeman barked at the dressing-gown, and the belt was hauled out from the loops. 'No plastic bags.' He pounced on the cotton-wool and sprawled it on the counter like the innards of some hygienic giant caterpillar. No pencil. No necklace. No nail scissors. No book. *The Charterhouse of Parma* joined bottles of contraband brandy and dagga in the police store-room.

I had been in the women's cells of Marshall Square once before, at the start of the 1956 Treason Trial, but the geography of the station was still bewildering. The corridors and court-yards we passed through were deserted. The murky passage led into a murkier cell. The cell door banged shut, and two more after it. There was only the bed to move towards.

What did They know? Had someone talked? Would their questions give me any clue? How could I parry the interrogation sessions to find out what *I* wanted to know, without giving them the impression that I was resolutely determined to tell them nothing? If I was truculent and delivered a flat refusal to talk to them at the very first session, they would try no questions at all, and I would glean nothing of the nature of their inquiry. I had to find a way not to answer questions, but without saying explicitly to my interrogators, 'I won't tell you anything'.

Calm but sleepless, I lay for hours on the bed, moving my spine and my legs round the bumps on the mattress, and trying to plan for my first interrogation session. Would I be able to tell from the first questions whether they knew I had been at Rivonia?* Had I been taken in on general suspicion of having been too long in the Congress movement, on freedom newspapers, mixing with Mandela and Sisulu, Kathrada and Govan Mbeki, who had been arrested at Rivonia, not to know something? Was it that the Security Branch was beside itself with rage that Joe had left the country – by coincidence one month before the fateful raid on Rivonia? Was I expected to throw light on why Joe had gone, on where he had gone? Had I been tailed to an illegal meeting? Had the police tumbled on documents typed on my typewriter, in a place where other revealing material had been found?

Or was I being held by the Security Branch not for interrogation at all, but because police investigations had led to me and I was being held in preparation for prosecution and to prevent me from getting away before the police were ready to swoop with a charge? At the first interrogation session, I decided, I would insist on saying nothing until I knew whether a charge was to be preferred against me. If I were asked whether I was willing to answer questions, I would say that I could not possibly know until I was given a warning about any impending prosecution. The Ninety-Day Law could be all things to all police. It could be used to extort confessions from a prisoner, and even if the confession could not – at the state of the law then – be used in court, it would be reassurance to the Security Branch that its suspicions were confirmed, and a signal to proceed with

* One month before my arrest, in July 1963, Security Police arrested Nelson Mandela and other political leaders in a raid on a house in the Johannesburg suburb of Rivonia. That house was used as the underground headquarters of the freedom struggle headed by the African National Congress. In what subsequently became known as the Rivonia Trial, Mandela and his associates were sentenced to terms of life imprisonment for directing sabotage and planning the armed overthrow of the South African Government.

a charge. My knowledge of the law was hazy, culled from years as a lawyer's wife only, and from my own experience of the police as a political organizer and journalist. Persons under arrest were entitled to the help of a lawyer in facing police questioning. If they would permit me no legal aid, I would tell them, whenever they came, that I would have to do the best I could helping myself. So I could not possibly answer any questions till I knew if the police were in the process of collecting evidence against me. Nor, for that matter, I decided to tell them, would I say that I would not answer questions. After all, how did I know that, until I knew what the questions were. If they would tell me the questions I would be in a better position to know what I would do. This cat-and-mouse game could go on for a limited period, I knew, but it was worth playing until I found out how the interrogation sessions were conducted, and whether there was any possibility that I might learn something of the state of police information. If they tired of the game, or saw through it – and this should not be difficult – I had lost nothing. Time was on their side anyway. If they showed their hand and revealed by intention or accident what they knew about my activities, I would have told them nothing, and I would be doubly warned to admit nothing. If fairly soon I was to be taken to court I would consider then, with the help of a lawyer, I hoped, the weight of the evidence against me. There was just a chance they might let slip some information, and even a chance – though it seemed remote the first night in the cell – that I might be able to pass it on to the Outside, to warn those still free.

As I dropped off to sleep the remembrance of that neatly folded but illegal copy of *Fighting Talk* rose again. If the best happened I would be released because there was no evidence against me ... and I would have withstood the pressure to answer questions ... but I would be brought to court and taken into prison for having one copy of a magazine behind the bottom shelf of a bookcase. How untidy! It would not make impressive reading in a news report.

*

I slept only to wake again. My ears knocked with the noise of a police station in operation. The cell was abandoned in isolation, yet suspended in a cacophony of noise. I lay in the midst of clamour but could see nothing. Accelerators raced, exhaust pipes roared, car doors banged, there were clipped shouted commands of authority. And the silence only of prisoners in intimidated subservience. It was Friday night, police-raid night. Pickup vans and *kwela-kwelas*,* policemen in uniform, detectives in plain clothes were combing locations and hostels, backyards and shebeens to clean the city of 'crime', and the doors of Marshall Square stood wide open to receive the haul of the dragnet.

Suddenly the noise came from the other side of the bed. Doors leading to other doors were opened, then one only feet away from mine, and I had for a neighbour, across the corridor, an unseen, disembodied creature who swore like a crow with delirium tremens.

'Water, water. *Ek wil water kry.* For the love of God, give me water.'

A violent retching, more shrieks for water, water. I caught the alcoholic parch and longed for water.

Twice again I was jerked awake by the rattle of doors to find the wardress standing in my doorway. She was on inspection, doing a routine count of the prisoners. 'Don't you ever sleep?' she asked.

Suddenly the door rattled open and a new wardress stared in. A tin dish appeared, on it a hard-boiled egg, two doorsteps of bread, and coffee in a jam-tin mug. Minutes later the crow was retreating down the passage. The wardress led me out of my cell, past a second solitary one, into the large dormitory cell which was divided by a half-wall from a cold water basin and a lavatory without a seat. I washed in cold-water and half a bucket of hot, put on my pyjamas and dressing-gown, was led out again into my little cell, and climbed back into bed. My first day in the police station had begun.

*

* The African name for pick-up vans. '*Kwela*' means 'jump', and this is the instruction that police shout at arrested Africans.

The Cell

I felt ill-equipped, tearful. I had no clothes. No daily dose of gland tablets (for a thyroid deficiency). My confiscated red suitcase, carefully packed from the accumulated experience of so many of us who had been arrested before, was the only thing, apart from me, that belonged at home, and in the suitcase were the comforts that could help me dismiss police station uniformity and squalor. I sat cross-legged on the bed, huddled against the cold, hang-dog sorry for myself.

The door clanged open and a lopsided gnome-like man said he was the Station Commandant. 'Any complaints?' he asked. This was the formula of the daily inspection rounds. I took the invitation. I objected to being locked up without charge, without trial, in solitary. The Commandant made it clear by his wooden silence that I was talking to the wrong man. The catalogue of complaints was for the record, I had decided. I would allow no prison or police official to get the impression that I accepted my detention. But the end of the recital that first morning tailed off on a plaintive note . . . 'and I've got none of my things . . . I want my suitcase, my clothes, my medicine. . . .'

'Where's her suitcase?' the Commandant demanded of the wardress, who passed the query on to the cell warder.

'Bring it. All of it. Every single thing.'

The cell warder went off at the double. Red suitcase appeared in the doorway, tied up with pink tape. The Station Commandant started to finger through it, then recoiled when he touched the underwear.

'She can have the lot!' he said.

The wardress, peering over his sloped left shoulder at the cosmetics, said shrilly: 'She can't have bottles. . . . The bottles . . . we can't have bottles in the cells.'

The Commandant rounded on her. One person would make the decisions, he told her. He had decided.

The cell warder retrieved the pink tape and the suitcase stayed behind in the cell. Nestling in it were an eyebrow tweezer, a hand mirror, a needle and cotton, my wrist-watch, all prohibited articles. And glass bottles, whose presence made the

17

wardresses more nervous than any other imagined contravention of the regulations, for it was a strict rule that nothing of glass should be allowed in the cells. I was later to find out why.

Throughout my stay in Marshall Square my suitcase was the difference between me and the casual prisoners. I lived in the cells; they were in transit. I had equipment, reserves. Their lipsticks were taken from them, and their combs, to be restored only when they were fetched to appear before a magistrate in court. The casuals were booked in from the police van in the clothes they had worn when arrested, and if they wanted a clean blouse they had to plead with the wardress to get the cell warder to telephone a relative. I could go to my suitcase. I had supplies. I was a long-termer in the cells.

There was a curious comfort about the first day. I had won my battle for the suitcase. I had made up my mind how I would try handling the Security Branch. Aloneness and idleness would be an unutterably prolonged bore, but it was early to worry about that, and for as long as I could, I would draw satisfaction from the time I had, at last, to think! Uninterruptedly, undistracted by the commands of daily living and working. The wardress on the afternoon shift seemed surprised I was taking it so quietly. 'You're catching up on your sleep,' she said. 'But soon the time will drag.'

I tried to translate noises into police station geography. There were three separate sets of rattlings before the wardress stood in my open doorway: there was a door that seemed to lead from the main part of the police station into the women's cells; about eight paces after that there was a door dividing the women's cells from a courtyard; and then there was my cell door. When I heard the first rattle of keys I could expect another two and the lapse of about fourteen paces before I lay in police view. Unless I was fast asleep I could not be pounced upon without warning. However quietly the wardress put the keys in the locks she could not hide her entry. The keys were too massive, the locks too stiff, the steel too ringing-loud. When I saw it I was transfixed by the largest of the keys, the one that opened the first door. Four and a half inches long, yet when I heard its rattle in the lock it seemed to grow in my mind's eye to the size of a poker.

The electric light burned constantly, day and night, but I could tell by the new wardress when it was a new night shift. As on the previous night I rehearsed again the imaginary first confrontation with the Security Branch. I was warming to my role in the encounter and was becoming master of the ambiguous and evasive reply to the questions I invented for my unseen interrogators.

I pushed out of my head a jumble of ideas and thoughts of people, with a deliberate resolve to think slowly, about one thing at a time, and to store up as much as I could for future days and nights. I postponed thinking about how I would try to pass the time. That, too, would be a subject for future hours. This was a time of emergency, and called for strict rationing.

I dropped off to sleep. There were the nightly inspections, the noisy intake of two drunks.

Right overhead, as though someone in the cell above had measured the spot where my head lay, a bottle broke sharply, and splintered on the concrete floor.

The next day was Sunday, but pandemonium. The cell door was flung open and the wardress, the cell warder, and a third policeman stared in, disbelievingly, I thought. There was prolonged shouting from the guts of the station, repeated banging of doors overhead. The Station Commandant had the door flung open a half-hour before the usual inspection. He said the usual 'Any complaints?' formula but was out of the cell before he could reply to my 'What about exercise?' The wardresses were tight-lipped, on edge. A fever seemed to rage in the working part of the police station, and the raised temperature flowed out to the prisoners lying in their cells.

There were four instead of two inspections that night. Trying to reconstruct the noises of the night hours I realized that there must have been an admission into the women's cells, and someone was in the cell opposite me, for there were two mugs of coffee in the hands of the morning-shift wardress.

Unexpectedly a high fastidious voice said 'I am due to menstruate, wardress, how do I get some cotton-wool?'

'Anne-Marie!' I shouted. 'Anne-Marie ... you here! Wardress, *I've* got cotton-wool.'

The cell doors opened long enough for me to pass out the cotton-wool and to catch a glimpse of Anne-Marie Wolpe – wife of our good friend Harold – haggard and drawn, perched on her high bed.

If Anne-Marie had been taken, Harold must have got safely away. The escape had come off, I decided. Thirty-six hours before I had gone into Marshall Square a break-out of the cells was being planned ...

*

Lying on his stomach on the floor of the upstairs cell Ninety-Day detainee Chiba had caught a fleeting glimpse of shapes and sizes under the crack in his door.

'Who's got ginger hair?' he called to Arthur Goldreich, who had played the role of flamboyant artist turned country squire by living in the Rivonia house and providing the front for the secret political work that went on in the outbuildings.

It was Harold Wolpe, brought in between policemen, in his red dyed hair and beard, caught at the Bechuanaland border where his escape bid had floundered, and locked up in Marshall Square with nightmarish fears over fingerprints and typewriters and sheets of paper in his handwriting.

'What've you done about an escape?' Harold asked Arthur in their first stolen conversation.

The two of them, and Indian Youth Congress activists Jassat and Mosie Moolla next door, used visits to the bathroom to haul themselves to the bars of the high w.c. window and count bricks to estimate the drop from the roof to wall, to the thick netting over the quadrangle of the women's jail, and down to the ground outside. Messages were smuggled out, and hacksaw blades smuggled in. Sawing sessions were conducted under cover of loud whistling and repeated pullings of the lavatory chain. Three minutes of sawing and the blades were blunt on the bars of tempered prison steel. Hacksaw blades continued to be inveigled into the cells, blades of every shape and size, the sawing continued, but the bars stood firm. It was young Mosie, with his charm, whom the young warder could not resist, and when Mosie broached the matter of an escape the policeman said he would cooperate as long as it would not appear that he had been an accomplice.

'No four men can overpower me, I'm as strong as a lion,' the warder said, so Arthur was instructed to practise blows with an iron bar and, all escape day, his stomach like jelly, he practised hitting his pillow with a bar, so as not to kill.

That night the four stuffed their beds with blanket rolls, put on their overcoats and stood waiting.

But four drunken drivers were being booked in downstairs and Operation Escape had to take second place to their examination by the district surgeon and the laboured issue of prisoners' property receipts to the four swaying new inmates of the cells.

The young warder appeared with the keys.

'Okay, Go!' he said, and stopped Arthur from trying a reluctant blow on his head. He would bang his own head against the wall, he had decided. Arthur walked rapidly out of his cell and knocked over a lemonade bottle. The four tiptoed out. On the corner of Main and Sauer Streets three bright lights spluttered and went out, with accomplice timing. The hacksaw blades were turfed into a rubbish-bin in the courtyard lined with empty Volkswagens. The four split up. Mosie and Jassat walked off towards the Indian residential area of Fordsburg; Arthur and Harold skirted the block desperately looking for the car that had not come. Two white down-and-outs tried to pick a fight with them. Arthur was piddling in a dark corner when the car eventually picked them up.

'Four 90-day Men Escape' *said the newspaper headlines.* 'Wives Held for Questioning'. *A massive police search for the fugitives followed.* 'Goldreich, described as the Security Branch's *major detainee, is still on the run. Police Patrols are at work throughout the land.' 'The police are being swamped with calls about the escapers.'*

'The Net Closes In'. '*A price of R1,000 is on the head of each escaper. Indian homes in the country districts of the Transvaal and homes and clubs in Johannesburg are being searched for the four.' 'Have you seen two European men and two Indian men walking together?' plain-clothes detectives were asking. Descriptions of the four were broadcast over the radio every twenty minutes at the climax of the manhunt, and all whites were enjoined to take part in the chase.*

For eleven days Arthur and Harold lived in darkness at a deserted house, eating raw bacon because the cooking made a sizzling noise; unable to use a heater because it gave off a red glow. The creak of a floorboard sounded, to their ears, like a revolver shot through the neighbourhood. By five o'clock each evening, dusk and a deep depression set in. 'Like being back in that cell,' said Harold.

Before each decision to act, tension mounted to breaking-point, but in movement and action there was relief. From one hiding-place to another, and then another. From cover in Johannesburg across the border into Swaziland. For six hours the two lay together under a tarpaulin. Then they could stretch, and move, stand up, and talk, and shout to the winds.

'Goldreich and Wolpe Escape to Francistown' *said the newspaper of 28 August. Minister Vorster said, 'They were two of our Biggest Fish'. They had been flown to Swaziland dressed as priests.*

In Francistown, Bechuanaland, at 4.15 one morning a knock on the window woke Goldreich: 'We've come to tell you your plane's been blown up.' The second chartered plane landed in Elizabethville with ten minutes' fuel to spare. . . . In the night-club black and white jived together to the blare of the band.

*

22

The Cell

In Marshall Square a new prisoner made his appearance in the men's exercise yard: a dimpled policeman, but stripped of his uniform.

A few hours after the escape, before he had time to claim his reward money, Johannes Arnoldus Greeff, only recently out of the Pretoria police training depot, broke down and confessed.

On his nineteenth birthday, Greeff's bid for bail was argued in court, and turned down, so the young policeman went back into the cells.

*

Dr Percy Yutar, it was obvious to all who encountered him during those months, coveted the job of State Prosecutor in the forthcoming Rivonia Trial. In an admiring circle of Security Branch detectives he was busy in the offices of The Grays, Security Branch headquarters in Johannesburg, poring over documents seized in police raids, and scrutinizing the recorded results of Ninety-Day detention victims. The Rivonia Trial was still some months off: the trial of Constable Johannes Arnoldus Greeff could be turned into a curtain-raiser.

Greeff was brought to trial on two charges: bribery and assisting four men to escape. His motive was really very simple. He had been hard-up. He had needed a pair of new shoes, cash to pay for motor-car repairs, more cash still. Half-way through the trial he changed his plea to guilty. The Marshall Square staff went to court to give evidence. After one policeman had stepped down from the witness-box, he looked across at the dock where Greeff stood, wearing a nervous smile throughout the trial, and winked at him. During court adjournments several policemen spoke to Greeff, the Press reports noticed, and gave him the thumbs-up sign of encouragement. But at his home in Rustenburg his mother locked away photographs of him. He had 'brought disgrace to the family,' she said. 'He has done something dishonourable.'

Dr Yutar said it was far more serious than that. This was a case of a young policeman 'fallen to the evil machinations of traitors who plotted a violent and hellish revolution in the country, planned on a military basis'. The State had a cast-iron case against those seized in the Rivonia raid, and their accomplices, now being rounded up. These persons would be brought to trial in time, the time of the Security Branch. Meanwhile Greeff was sentenced to six years' imprisonment.

Chapter Two

ON LIVING IN A POLICE STATION

Anne-Marie was taken out of her cell. Hurriedly. 'The magistrate is waiting,' the wardress, accompanied by the sergeant, shouted. When lunch was brought, the cell opposite was still empty. Then Anne-Marie reappeared, only to bundle up her clothes, and be marched out again. That was the last I saw of her.

Three men in plain clothes were ushered into my cell. They ran their hands up and down the walls, looked hard at the window, withdrew. All day the cell opened and closed. And much of that night, and the next.

All week the police station was in frenzied disarray. Heads would fall. But whose? Prisoners or policemen? Marshall Square, central police station in the country, was in disgrace. Authority was sitting on the problem. The Security Branch was running a manhunt. The country joined in the game, for everyone loves an escape and an official scandal, and the two together were enormously satisfying – for outsiders.

But in Marshall Square there was an ominous atmosphere of revenge and reprisals. Some official action was imminent, but nothing was announced. The station brooded, and waited, and we, its prisoners, with it.

Still the cell doors opened and closed. The heads of the Johannesburg District Police Command came to inspect us, the doors, the windows, the lay-out of the police station. A colonel, then a major, followed by a brigadier. A pause of half a day, then two Public Works Department men, their African labourer hovering in the background, then the P.W.D. supervisor. Throughout the night Big Brass continued to swoop on the station, insisting on a cell-by-cell inspection. Gold braid and pale blue cap bands appeared at the door in Technicolor parade. 'Any complaints?' they asked, for they had to say something. 'I want to be released,' I replied from cover of the blankets, and

25

the officers chortled in their throats to their inferiors, or stared in disbelief.

On the fourth day I asked the little Station Commandant about exercise.

'Exercise! That'll have to wait. Can't you see this place is in a *dinges*?'*

'A *dinges*?' I pretended not to understand.

'Oh, all right, a turmoil then,' and he added, ominously 'After this things are going to be tough, very tough. You've seen nothing yet.' He was half out of the door, '. . . and you'd better get rid of those bottles!'

'Slovo!' There was the rattle of keys and the door clanged open.

'Goldreich!' Suddenly there was gentle Hazel, Arthur's wife, and we blinked delightedly at one another in the sun. The wardress set off in the direction of the men's exercise yard, and Hazel and I pranced behind her, mouthing enthusiastic welcomes to one another. Too soon we reached the exercise yard where a Security Branch photographer had his camera and flash gun poised, and list of detainees. While I had my picture taken, my back against the brick wall, Hazel peered at the list. 'Anne-Marie's been released,' she hissed, spotting on the list next to A. Wolpe the word '*ontslaan*' [released].

'*Ai* . . . *aai* . . . they're together . . . they're together!' The Station Commandant had come into the yard and leapt into the air in a series of panicky jerks at the sight of Hazel and me together. The wardress was flummoxed. She had been told to bring Slovo and Goldreich to the photographer. Those had been Security Branch instructions, after all, and no one had explicitly said, 'But not the two of them together.' Back we were hustled, individually, into our cells. But the encounter had taken place and though precautions against our seeing one another were stricter than ever, we knew we had company beyond the courtyard wall, and the presence of someone else in the same predicament was selfishly reassuring.

* Afrikaans slang for 'what-d'ye-call-it'.

26

Soon the little Commandant came on no more inspections. The new chief appeared. A police captain, he had been transferred to this post to tighten security, and this was promotion for him. He wore his cap during inspections and carried his swagger stick under his arm. The salutes of the cell warder were smarter, the wardresses stood up straighter.

'What's going on?' I asked a wardress.

'We're not allowed to talk to you,' she snapped.

Two white workers and three Africans moved in with an oxy-acetylene machine. To the roar of the petrol motor and blinding, flying blue sparks, they began a drilling operation on the outside of my cell door and the one opposite. I heard them at work on Hazel's door in the outside courtyard. At last, a major policy decision had been reached at police headquarters. Four prisoners had bolted, and so the remaining prisoners held for interrogation were to have double locks on their doors, and triple locks if the doors were already double-locked. Spitting forks of flame the oxy-acetylene machine cut great cavities in the doors of the women's section and was then heard roaring away overhead on the first floor. Then followed a locksmith who fastened a thick bolt and bar lock over the outside of the doors. At last the full purpose of the Plan became clear. A new warder made his appearance on the next morning shift. In addition to the usual keys he held a great new bunch, each key accompanied on the ring by a yellow metal number disc. This warder's sole job was to guard the second key to the cells of the politicals. The wardresses still had their keys: one to the women's jail, one to the inner courtyard, one to the cells. But without the Key Man the wardresses could not reach us. When food was brought, if we fell ill in the night, when we needed to go to the toilet, when the Station Commandant came on inspection, if the Security Branch wanted to interview us, the Key Man had to be there to open up.

At meal times the Key Man was frantic, rushing from cells upstairs to those downstairs to turn his rows of locks. The bar lock was to be closed tight in front of his eyes. He had a grave personal and official responsibility to see that the politicals were locked tight in their cells. His presence was a constant admonition to the warders that one of their number had defected. The keys in the hands of the wardresses, once a badge of office, had become a mockery. The wardresses locked the prisoners in their cells, but were themselves powerless to regulate their incarceration. They had degenerated into skivvies, into messengers sent to fetch a man carrying a key ring. 'I want to go to the toilet,' I would cry if the wardress was in earshot. 'I'll have to see if I can get the keys,' the wardress would shout grumpily, and set off to badger the Key Man to open this door before any other. When the wardresses were not cursing the slowness of the Key Man in coming, they grumbled about the constable who had let the whole force down. 'That bloody Greeff! What did he think he was doing? And he didn't even get the escape money in the end. . . .'

The Key Man was, conceivably, in a respected position of trust. The locked doors had always been impenetrable; the heavy bar locks burned into the steel door merely reinforced their impenetrability. It was human frailty, not steel, that had proved vincible. One policeman had now been set over all the others. Big Brother, hauled from the ranks, was watching them. But all he did was turn keys in locks, at the beck and call of those who might have yielded to temptation, and the smugness in being a repository of headquarters' trust soon became a disgruntled boredom.

For my part, I found myself slipping with disconcerting ease into a dreary, squalid routine of locked-up life in an airless, grimy concrete space. My cell was solitary, By Order. Too small, anyway, to take a second prisoner. There was no one to make police-cell conversation with: Why are you here? Have you been in before? Do you think you will get off? (*Never*: Did you do it. . .?) . . . Oh, me? Political. Ninety days. What's that, you said? I was trying to turn isolation into an advantage. But the clang of the steel, the doors without handles, the never-ending inspections were constant physical reminders of the humiliation of being locked away.

There were other such reminders. Slap centre in the cell door was the penny-sized peephole. By prison standards it was designed to have the prisoner under scrutiny from the outside, not for the prisoner to view anything from the inside of the cell. 'Back from the door!' the wardress would cry when she saw the pupil of an eye up against the peephole. The hole was hers, to see if the prisoner was on the bed or off it. Sitting up or lying down. Laughing or crying. Facing the wall or turned away from it. Alive or dead. Locked up or escaped. I resented the spyhole and felt that to be peered at through it was a violent infringement of my privacy. Above all I objected to being talked to through the hole. 'If you want to see if I'm here, or say anything to me,' I told the police and the wardresses, 'Open the door. Don't spy at me through that hole.' I hated the night inspections when officers came from the police barracks and sidled up to the peephole to see for themselves. Some of the wardresses shared my indignation for reasons of their own prudery. If men warders wanted to see women prisoners, they said, they should ask the wardress to unlock the door and herself see if it was 'safe' for a man to look. Only then should the officer be invited to make his inspection. (The Key Man, it was implied, should open the door with his eyes closed.) I used the peephole when I needed to identify movement in the narrow passage outside my cell. Perhaps another political was being brought in, someone I might know. I might read in the expression of a detainee whether she had faced a gruelling interrogation; whether she had learned anything along that prison grapevine that gave so little to the politicals in isolation. When I saw the faces and walk of the ordinary prisoners I could tell much more about them from the sounds they made. The wardress did not need to see the pupil of my eye to know I was on tiptoe peering through. My eye would block the narrow shaft of light through the hole, and she would know. I felt humiliated every time I was detected standing on tiptoe trying to look out. It was as though my curiosity had got the better of my ability to exist in isolation.

Isolation and privacy. Not the same thing by any means. I was isolated, but utterly dependent on outsiders – my jailers, my enemies. I had to shout or bang on the door when I wanted to use the lavatory. The wardress stood by while I washed. The daily programme, whatever I pretended, was not mine but theirs.

Prison routine imposed itself during the first days of bewildered existence in blackness. The electric light burned endlessly but showed nothing but the end of my bedstead, and beyond that, my red suitcase enthroned on the wall shelf. I could dispense with my eyes. Ears were more useful in isolation. There would be the jingle of keys and the clang of doors to announce the approach of an intruder, or a new episode in the regulated monotony of life in a cell.

I identified the wardresses by the sound of them long before I saw them. Female voices. Raucous. Shrill. Pained. Competent ('I know my job. I don't lose control but don't think you can get the better of me'). In time Raucous and Shrill personalized into the two ugly sisters among the wardresses. Raucous was stupid as a stone, and as deaf. She knew by rote the mechanical duties of a wardress. Inspections at intervals by night and by day. Carry in the food. Remove the plates after some time. Get the Key Man to unlock the door for the captain's inspection. Watch the prisoner at exercise. Search the body of the newly admitted prisoner. No money, watches, or jewellery. Confiscate pills, sharp instruments, glass bottles. Hand out blankets and keep count of those in store. Send used blankets for fumigation. Walk behind the prisoner in case she attacks you from behind. No talking by politicals in isolation. But Raucous was deaf, so she had to watch the mouths of the detainees, and on the way to the wash basin you might snatch a word with the prostitutes or drunks in the large cell, and then pretend you had been singing.

Shrill had a face like an underdone crumpled crumpet, with eyes as expressive as a fish moth's, and apart from highly polished floors and a little property she owned on a sixth of an acre in Parkhurst, she knew no passion in life.

Pained was a handsome Wagnerian blonde, with long elegant hands, but feet crippled by bunions. Her aches and twinges might have been an excuse for her long-suffering voice and expression, and for her treatment of all prisoners as inveterate nuisances, if it were not that everything that happened, to her and in general, was sent to try her already unbearable martyrdom. When it rained it was because her bunions would ache harder. If there were prisoners to be admitted it was because they knew it was her shift. Prostitutes were not only law-breakers, but a deliberate affront to her sex. Two husbands had been snatched from her – by death, also devised to try her – before either marriage had lasted longer than a few years. All remaining men were repulsively scheming. It was Pained who suggested that the wardresses make a private arrangement to begin their evening shifts before the official time to cut down the chances of her being intercepted by men on the walk through Johannesburg from the bus stop to the police station. Pained spent hours neglecting her duties in the women's cells to lean over the counter in the charge office where there was male conversation. From each eavesdropping session she returned repelled but freshly fascinated, convinced she had made a batch of new conquests, but determined to repulse every one of them.

Raucous was too stupid to think of her prisoners as anything but ciphers, and to remember the total she was currently responsible for. Shrill had no time to think about persons : the floor could always be made to shine more brightly. Pained concentrated on her feet and protecting herself from imaginary attacks by men, and competition from women. As for Competent, she was interested in people, even kind to them, but while she could handle drunks without provoking them, and prostitutes and shoplifters as creatures fallen by the wayside whom magistrates in their wisdom would correct with a spell behind bars, politicals were completely beyond her. We looked like any respectable middle-class women, and seemed better educated and better spoken than most. We seemed amenable to prison discipline yet we were locked up by the Security Branch as darkly dangerous to the survival of the State. The wardresses were under strict instructions not to talk to us, and after the escape these instructions were reissued in more emphatic form.

Competent had been too long at Marshall Square to be awed by new regulations or new superiors. She talked to us when she felt like it, and she talked about the subjects she judged safe : the plot of the latest film at the Colosseum, an article in the *Reader's Digest*, Royal Family marriages and babies. She was an Afrikaner but had married an English policeman of the force some forty years before. All the wardresses were 'police widows'. Their husbands had died or been killed in the service. They had inherited their police station jobs as compensation, and together with the jobs an air of martyrdom (Our Husbands gave their Lives to the Force), and a blind loyalty. The police are always right, all police are right. The law is the law, and that is that. To criticize the racial nature of the law or the use of the police to enforce it is to insult a policeman's mother or his religion. The dingy police stations keep the sacred flame of racism burning in countless outposts throughout the country.

Marshall Square is the most important police station in South Africa's largest city. Busy nights are Fridays and Saturdays when the station becomes a sounding board for the meanest aspects of city life. The Ninety-Dayers were locked away from this mainstream of police station life, but the sounds and some of the sights washed us nevertheless. Washed and were welcome in a series of endless days when time was determined only by the scratches on the wall and the visits of Security Branch interrogators. The politicals were in separate cells, segregated from the other prisoners, but sounds filtered through the thick walls, especially at night when the roar of the traffic died down. Several times a day I was ushered to the washroom of the large communal cell next door and though, if there were other prisoners there, the wardress stood on duty to make sure I did not try to communicate with them, she couldn't stop me from seeing them and associating them with the sounds I thought I had heard them make during the night. Through the cells, over the months I was there, a procession of women moved, some of the early-comers reappearing in the queue towards the end of my term to be greeted familiarly if not warmly by the wardresses. Others made a frightened first acquaintance with the cell and I watched their reactions, identical with mine, to the decaying smell of the blankets, the primitive toilet arrangements and the bleakness of days and nights behind bars. There was the little woman in green and fawn voile, so frail-looking, who fainted when she was allocated her prison bed; she was in for shoplifting and the evidence of her crime was a tin of powdered milk and a packet of biscuits. Two women came in together: a hardfaced young blonde and a pretty dark girl with the posture of a ballet dancer. They were charged with robbery. The blonde had held a cosh over the head of the elderly jeweller to give her gang time to make a get-away. The dark girl was the girl-friend of one of the gang members, an Italian called Angelo, and he had been arrested in her flat. Angelo was upstairs in the men's cells and each evening, when the shifts were changing over, the dark girl climbed on the toilet bowl to talk to him, through two sets of barred windows. It broke his heart, he shouted down to her at the top of his voice, that his girl should be pregnant with his baby in jail. If the baby were a boy they would call him Marshall, and if a girl her name would be Square. The blonde and the dark girl were the best of friends. They wound one another's hair in curlers and shared paperback romances. But every now and then the blonde was called out by the detective in charge of the case: for 'further investigation', it was said. Unknown to the dark girl the blonde was cooperating with the police in exchange for an undertaking to escape prosecution.

Most of the women in the cells were prostitutes and drunks. Sometimes they were both: prostitutes who were heavy drinkers and had lost any good looks they might have had in the tough life of keeping a ponce on their earnings.

The most faithful frequenters of the Marshall Square cells were those women grown too dissipated to attract any regular custom and who had become drunk hobos littering the parks and the library gardens in dirty, dishevelled, diseased, and wretched groups. These sherry-gangers, as they are known in Johannesburg and in Durban where they spend their winter sojourn, were scooped into the police vans regularly, wearing their tight hair curlers, men's jackets, sand shoes and bandages on their sore legs like a uniform. They were charged with loitering or appearing drunk in a public place, served a few weeks or months and then filtered back to their old haunts, only to be arrested again when the pick-up vans did their regular Friday night clean-up of the city parks.

The drunks invariably made a clamorous entry. Then either they slid into a stupor within minutes of being locked up, or they roared away half the night. Much depended on how the wardresses handled them. Left to themselves the roar would eventually subside to a whimper, though that might take a few hours. Shrill could not leave them alone, she seemed to think it was a dereliction of duty not to shout threats at a drunk, but the more she scolded the harder the drunk swore and raged. One night her piercing threats infuriated a woman already heavily incited by the bottle and Shrill had no sooner withdrawn from the cells after a vigorous imprecation against 'you rubbish' when there was a loud crash and a sound of splintering glass on the concrete floor. Then silence. I could not imagine what the woman next door had done. There was nothing I could do to summon Shrill: the heavy doors between the cells and the office of the wardress blocked all sound, and once the wardress had withdrawn we could not call her back, we could only lie and wait till her own sense of duty brought her round sooner or later. This time it was sooner. Shrill came back, probably to have another go at the drunk's expense, but when she opened the door of the large cell and looked inside she hastily re-locked and fled shouting for help to the charge office. Three constables hurried in as reinforcements. The drunk had hurled a large enamel mug at the naked light bulb high in the ceiling; she had hit target first shot; and had then used a piece of the splintered glass on her arm. The attempt to sever an artery had been half-hearted, and though there was blood to be seen, I gathered from the policemen's talk that the cut was superficial and the drunk was already recovering from her frenzy. But not if Shrill could prevent it. She insisted that the woman be put in a strait-jacket. The constables deferred to her, for the women prisoners were her responsibility. As she could not manage the operation alone they waited for her to fetch the jacket and then set to work to force the woman into it. For the three of them acting in concert it was an easy enough exercise; they laughed and joked as they went to work. The woman was in a paroxysm of fury, but not drunk fury any longer. 'I'm not mad, I'm not mad, don't put me in this thing,' she sobbed, and then, 'It's too tight, you're pulling the arms too tight, I can't breathe,' but as the struggling minutes went by she shouted no more, and she was left trussed up on the mattress which had been dragged off the bed and on to the floor. I had lain listening to this with a sick feeling in my stomach and shivers in my limbs. The constables were chattering and joking as they left, with Shrill bringing up the triumphant rear. There was silence for a while, then a steady hard drumming on the door of the next cell. It took me some time to work it out, but I realized that the woman had moved like a crab on her back from the mattress on the floor and had manoeuvred herself to the door and was using her legs to drum on it in continued protest. Some hours later Shrill brought the constables back to remove the strait-jacket; 'Perhaps,' she told the woman, 'you've learnt your lesson by now.'

Friday nights were inferno-like, especially at month-end when pensions were paid and the disabled-turned-drunks spilled from the benches in the parks into the vans. On the pavement outside Marshall Square the pick-up van doors clanged open and shut and roared off for another swoop. Africans were herded into the charge office to shouts of '*Kom aan, Kom aan*' [Come on, Get a move on] and the sherry-gangers howled and swore through the night, till the shouts turned into gravel-sounding alcoholic snores and it was time to eat the dry bread and hard-boiled egg and join the queue to court.

The courts sat at 9.30 each morning but the station regulations insisted that the women be got ready for their court appearance fully three hours before. Many of them did need time to sober up; perhaps they did this faster sitting in rows on a hard bench than in their cell beds. If they were new to this experience the women would do an agitated smoothing of their crumpled clothes and hair while rehearsing before anyone in earshot, prisoner or wardress, the explanation they would offer to the Bench of how they of all people had been arrested. The old-timers took it for granted that they should periodically serve a spell in prison. They speculated on which magistrate would be on the Bench, the mood he was likely to be in, and the sentence he would impose in view of previous sentences and warnings. For all the need of the uninitiated to rehearse and the fund of experience the old hands could draw on, the early morning period dragged slowly.

This was the time the station slowed down to half-speed. If the pick-up vans knew their business they would deliver no new admissions to the charge office because the court lists for the day had already been made up. You could hardly receipt a prisoner and his property only to hand him over to new court cell custodians in return for a fresh set of receipts, without a decent lapse of time to allow for the laborious insertion of the sheets of carbon paper, the licking of the indelible pencil, and the careful count and re-count of human stock. In any event, Marshall Square staff was changing over and the departure of the old and the arrival of the new shift was a major trauma in the life of the station.

Once the prisoners had been shunted off to court and the new shift had taken over the cells, the station could get down to the serious business of the day: cleaning up. The wardresses who came on duty did not seem to notice the prisoners in the cells. We might not have existed. It would have been better at this time if we had not: I am sure that if the wardresses had any attitude to Ninety-Day detention it was that our uninterrupted occupation of the cells, without a decent exit in the crocodile of the prisoners being taken to Court, obstructed a really good polish. For cleaning meant the floors. The windows were not cleaned; the years of accumulation of sticky grime on the bars went untouched. Except rarely the basin and the lavatory were not properly cleaned: the budget of the station did not run to the right equipment and cleaners. But the floors, ah the floors . . .

The morning-shift wardress signed on, read the occurrence

book, took off her hat, and made a dive for the African cells. There, her shrieks mingling with the shouts of the warders, white and black, she chose her quota of labour. Not too many youngsters, they couldn't supply the elbow grease. Not that one. He looks 'cheeky'. Five or six awaiting-trial African prisoners in tow, the wardress would fetch a motley collection of already filthy polishing cloths, remnants of torn prison blankets. The arrival of the work party in the women's cells, when Raucous or Shrill were on shift, could have provided the sound-track for the arrival of the damned in apartheid hell. Both these wardresses shouted instructions uninterruptedly in Afrikaans. In South African police stations the assumption, never questioned, is that all African prisoners must understand and speak Afrikaans if they know what is good for them. A further assumption is that every prisoner knows police station routine and the quixotic preferences, on the floor-polishing stint, of every wardress. The floors were concrete, polished to a high, bright red with a cheap polish. First a sweeping, then an application of the polish in lumps at strategic points, then a good hard rub. Now the fun started. The wardress would shriek 'cha-cha' or 'twist'. The prisoner had to station his two legs on two cleaning rags and move to the beat called by the wardress. (What did they do before the cha-cha? Did the waltz and the foxtrot rhythms do as well for the floors?) Shrill had a rather individual approach to the floors. She apportioned each prisoner to a large square of the cement and their cha-cha sway was ordered not to infringe the borders of any neighbouring square. Raucous was persecuted by water stains which showed up strongly on the floor surface, and each spot had to get special rubbing treatment by a carefully designated prisoner. The noisy swaying pantomime could go on for fifteen minutes in an individual cell.

I, a prisoner held under top security conditions, was forbidden books, visitors, contact with any other prisoner; but like any white South African Madam I sat in bed each morning, and Africans did the cleaning for the 'missus'. Should a spot appear on the floor during the day the wardress would shout to the nearest African warder '*Gaan haal my 'n kaffer*' [Go and get me a kaffir], and once again all would be well in South Africa's forced labour heaven. All the prisoners in Marshall Square (except the Ninety-Day detainees) were prisoners awaiting trial and as such protected by prison regulations from having to do any work other than keep their own cells clean. They were in most cases probably ignorant of this right. Those who knew of it seemed to judge it politic to feign ignorance, except for the rare cases of men who, when called for cha-cha duty, said flatly that they were not willing to work. This happened only twice during my stay. It gave the wardresses something to talk about and indignation at 'cheeky kaffirs' rose stridently when Pained and Raucous changed shift and exchanged station news.

The African prisoners soon got the measure of the wardresses. When Competent was on duty they worked fast and chattered softly under their breaths. They indulged in uproarious mime of Raucous and Shrill, imitating the straddled walk of the first and the explosive inarticulateness of the second when she tried to discipline them. When the haul the night before had been of young *tsotsis*,* cleaning sessions were scenes of wild disorder. When older men had been arrested they arrived neat in sports-jackets and pressed trousers, or in the ridiculous short-trouser-legged uniform of the domestic worker, and resignedly took up the polishing cloths in weary acceptance that this was the lot of the man whose pass-book was not in order or whose bad luck it was to run up against the police over some misdemeanour or other. The cleaning session was a chance to get out of the cooped-up communal African cells on the other side of the building, and an opportunity to check on the police station talk that in the women's cells were sitting well-dressed Madams equipped with suitcases, pillows and thermos flasks, as though they had fallen on bad days and had to accept installation in a police station cell rather than in a mean and disreputable boarding-house.

For the wardresses the progress of the cleaning set the mood

* Strictly speaking, a young African delinquent, but whites use this term for any African youngster who wears flashy clothes.

of the day. When there was a crowded cell of African awaiting-trial prisoners the floors sparkled well in time for the Commandant's morning inspection and the wardresses were light-hearted at their achievement. One morning the routine got off to a sluggish start. There seemed to be more than the usual hullabaloo at the other end of the station. When the wardress appeared her face was black. 'We're short of a prisoner,' she snapped. My heart jumped in spontaneous sympathy for any prisoner bold and resourceful enough to get out of the police station, *and* so soon after the Goldreich–Wolpe–Moolla–Jassat escape and counter-measures. But it was not another escape, just that the night's catch had been bad and the wardress had been short of one man to make up the minimum complement of her cleaning squad.

Every morning as the cha-cha cleaners were on their way out, the wardress on duty would thrust a large aluminium bucket at one and order him to bring hot water for the 'missus'. That was me. Washing in a bucket was the highlight of my day. The hot water would rub away the mouldy blanket smell that pervaded the cell, and when the bucket was brought I would accept with alacrity the invitation to be locked in the large communal cell that sported the wash-basin. The bucket of hot water was a concession to the Ninety-Dayers' permanent residence in the cells; the ordinary occupants had to manage under the cold water tap. For the first few days I grappled with the water in the bucket unsuccessfully. To pour it over me would have been a wonderful splurge but of few seconds' duration. If I stood in the bucket it would be like an uncomfortable stork, more out of the water than in it. In time I improvised a bath by acrobatics. I poured the water into the basin and perched on it in an inelegant squat, face and stomach towards the wall, legs dangling. Then I poured water over myself with cupped hands. It made a great splash that sounded like fun if anyone cared to listen, and I knew that the prisoners would hold the pools of water on the floor against, not me, but the wardress if they were called in to do a second mopping.

Bath over, it was the start of a new day, another day of torpid inactivity. Lying in bed at night could be excused as a retreat from inactivity. Lying in bed by day had to be an activity in itself, and each hour spent lying flat on my back or leaning against the propped pillow was an exercise in trying to cajole a state of resigned semi-consciousness out of myself.

The cell was too small to move in; it was cold and futile to stand on the floor; I lived on the bed. From the bed I made scratches with a hairpin on the wall next to my head. Each scratch took me at most 120 seconds to make, but I had to await the passage of 1,440 minutes, or 86,400 seconds, before I could make the next. How many marks would I have to make before I got out of this cell?

Life outside was so close and yet inaccessible. On my iron bedstead I lay in the centre of the busiest city in Africa. The external wall of my cell stood on the corner of Marshall and Sauer Streets and all day the traffic hooted and the crowds milled around me, but we were invisible to one another. Several times a day I held a clean tissue in each hand to grip the bars in squeamish distaste at the grime thickly coating them, and I strained on my toes on the bedstead to see out of the window high in the wall. The figures rushing past could have been on celluloid film; they were not part of my world. The businessmen hurrying into the Danish restaurant opposite (I had eaten there myself in other times) spared an hour for their *hors-d'œuvre* and poached trout, then bolted back to their desks, telephones, and ticker-tape. I was not hungry; I did not deny the diners their food, but I developed an antagonism towards those men in well-tailored suits who could bustle into the restaurant without turning their heads to the grilles in the grimy building opposite and whose complacency, I told myself, was a clear complicity.

I was watching the after-dinner rush back to the offices one day when I made an exciting discovery. A bustle on the pavement diametrically opposite my grille disclosed an African newspaper vendor setting up shop on the paving-stones. He moved with careful deliberation to stack the papers against the wall behind him, removed the thick twine and cardboard coverings, stuffed those into a refuse basket and then, wonder of all wonders, drew folded sheets from the bundle on top of the stack and prepared to wrap the afternoon paper's news poster round the pole of an electric light standard. It was winter and he had to wrestle with the wind, but he got the poster up and then withdrew to the business of selling out his edition. The poster was to catch the eye of potential purchasers, of course, and so he had swivelled it round on the pole to lie in view of the pedestrians moving towards him on his pavement. Perhaps if he had known I was craning my neck from the cell window over the road he might not have hung the poster so that two-thirds of the letters faced directly away from my gaze. To me it looked like this:

QUA

I

RHO

RHO had to be Rhodesia. But what in Rhodesia? Quarrel? Newspaper posters were getting vaguer than ever. Qualms? Ditto. Quads? Well, I suppose so, but they must have been special to merit a poster. (It never struck me that it was a QUAKE in Rhodesia. I had never thought of Rhodesia as earthquake-prone.)

I strained my neck muscles daily trying to get a hint of the news from the poster. Sometimes it was hung completely out of my line of vision. Once I thought I saw something like SABO, which could only mean SABOTAGE, but I did not know if it had been a successful attempt or a successful piece of police detection. Knowing the posters were on the pole opposite and seeing the stacks of newspapers I felt more in touch with the news, but at the end of weeks shinning up the bars and craning my neck I had to admit that I had culled disappointingly little from the pole. Still, I went on trying. I called it reading my daily newspaper.

The Security Branch detective had jeered 'Bye-bye, blue sky' as he handed me over to the police station. He was wrong. I did see the sky, but through a canopy of barbed wire. That was over a week after my arrest. The excitement of the escape still simmered through the station but routine reasserted itself, and one day when the cell door opened it was not to admit yet another arm of the law but to let me out. One hour's exercise daily. Alone. I was to spend the hour in the bricked-in quadrangle of the women's section of the brick and bar monster that is Marshall Square. Part of the building goes back to pre-Boer War days. The plumbing pipes are all external and they lace the walls of the quadrangles like a corset of iron trellis. Water and sewage pipes gurgle and splutter and flush up and down the two storeys and this little exercise yard is an excellent point from which to plot an ablutions graph for the white prisoners' cells. The few steps out of the cell were like a hurtle through space on a fun-fair figure of eight, and my stomach leapt as my legs moved across the concrete threshold. But the exercise yard was too like a cell. The sky was trapped by brick walls extending upwards and, like the warders regulating my stay in the court-yard, the brick walls officiously limited the shine of the sun. There was nothing for it but to walk round and round the courtyard.

On chill days I loped but tried to put out of my mind the thought of generations of prisoners doing the same. On sunny days I basked in the patch of sun, moving with it, if I could stay long enough, as it inched westwards across the courtyard and then out of reach.

There was another exercise yard for the women but it was used for men detainees until the women wardresses reasserted their, or our, claim. This was a sandy yard, four times the size of the women's quadrangle, deep in the bowels of the station and closed in by fourteen-feet-high brick walls, with mesh on top. To see what lay beyond the walls I stood in the pit of the quadrangle with my head thrown back. Then like a victim in the gladiators' den I could see and be seen by the elevated spectators, in this case the skyscrapers of Johannesburg's mining and finance houses. Marshall Square lies in the heart of the multi-millionaire concerns mining South Africa's gold and diamonds. The new Chamber of Mines building is a stone's throw away.

On Living in a Police Station

Anglo-American's twin giants, number 44 and number 45 Main Street, are paces away. The Stock Exchange is on the next block. The windows looking down on me were those of panelled board rooms and offices housing smooth desk-tops. I judged feeling on the Ninety-Day detention clause by whether the clerk sorting papers in the office which had a ringside seat on my arena raised his head or hand in answer to my cheery, seemingly unconcerned wave, or stared down in haughty disdain. If it was a lunch-hour, groups of girls would pass along the windowed corridor and one might catch sight of me and call the others to stare and stare. Did they know what they were looking at? Did they care?

The large exercise yard had other diversions. On the blistering green paint of the yard door was the detainees' register. The first Ninety-Dayers had seen the scratched initials and cupid's hearts that decorate every blank police station space. Next to *Edith Loves Vic for Ever*, Wolfie Kodesh had scratched *W.K. Loves Freedom for Ever*. Leon Levy had quoted Vorster's words to Parliament: *Ninety days ... or eternity ...*. He had added four question marks. Mosie Moolla and Jassat had scratched their names. Lilian Ngoyi, Kumalo, Molefe, Tsele, Kunene and Dhlamini were there. Arthur Goldreich had written his and Hazel's name in his precise architectural printing; Harold was there too. The large exercise yard had become our place of reunion and our archive. Next to the names were scratched the dates of detention, and simple arithmetic calculations deduced that the fate of those arrested was continuous detention, except for those who had escaped or left the country.

One morning there were freshly scratched letters on the door. The sight of the name chilled me. James Kantor was detained in Marshall Square. James Kantor, from Monday to Friday attorney, in the courts and corridors of the magistrate's court, at week-ends socialite yachtsman on Hartebeespoort Dam, was locked in the cells which had held countless clients he had defended on charges of theft and robbery, fraud, soliciting, and assault. James Kantor was Harold Wolpe's brother-in-law.

43

His arrest was more than pique at Harold's escape; this was ugly reprisal action against a political innocent, the taking of hostages, Kantor for Wolpe.

We who chose to be involved in politics did not, could not, define the reaches of Government counter-action. The Ninety-Day law recognized no demarcation of its territory, no delimiting of its power. All were within its grasp, and the possibilities of its use to intimidate and destroy both the committed and the innocent on the sidelines were more frightening than I had realized.

Other new names appeared on the prisoners' roster, names I had never heard before. That proved that the forces opposed to the Government were stronger than I had thought; it showed, too, that the Government was still mounting its offensive. Were we withstanding the attack? What was going on outside the prisons, in the streets, the townships, the secret meetings? In prison you see only the moves of the enemy. Prison is the hardest place to fight a battle.

One morning in the second week I had barely had time to get used to being outside the cell when the wardress appeared to usher in a neat little man with white hair, shiny starched white shirt, white hands holding a sheet of white paper. The magistrate was paying his weekly call. Any complaints? he asked. I had been complaining endlessly. I intended to permit no one the illusion that I accepted my imprisonment with resignation. I was in a state of buoyant aggression, disarmed of weapons except for the last, my tongue. I complained to the Big Wigs who came on nocturnal inspections. They said nothing or 'humpff' and brushed off my rush of words as coming from an intransigent trouble-maker and no wonder the Security Branch locked *her* up, look at the way she never stops complaining. I complained to the wardresses who said, 'You'll get more out of them if you don't complain so much.' I complained to the nicer policemen who said they were only doing their jobs, and *they* hadn't locked me up. Some said, 'We don't make the laws, you know.' One said, admiringly, 'She's a fighter.' That was the

44

morning I had a row with the wardress who did not bring me
the bucket of hot water till half past ten. I complained to the
Station Commandant who said it was none of his affair, I
should tell the Security Branch, or the magistrate.

The magistrate stood before me, pencil poised. Did he
know, I demanded, what it was like to be locked up with
nothing to do, nothing to read, no one to see? Did he know
what it was like to be detained without knowing why, or for
how long? Did he not agree that the Ninety-Day detention law
was callous, cruel, inhuman? I don't know what he wrote of my
rhetorical questions, but the pencil moved conscientiously
across the paper. The magistrate said almost nothing. He would
convey what I said to the Minister. He said this each time and
each time that he returned it was without any reply. I bullied
the little man outrageously. He did not cut me short, or refer
my complaints to someone else. How could he? His appoint-
ment was the one 'concession' – and a useless one it turned out
to be – that the Minister had made to criticism in Parliament of
his No-Trial law. So the magistrate listened and wrote, and his
notes, when typed out, turned up on the desk of the Security
Branch interrogator about whose arbitrary control I was complaining, for the direction of the work both of the magistrates
and the Security Branch falls under the Department of Justice.
The Minister makes the law, orders his officials to execute it,
and pretends to use his magistrates to act as watchdogs against
its abuses.

The little magistrate did the best he could, which was to listen
carefully and write painstakingly. When the flow of complaints
ceased – and their tenor was always more or less the same – 'I
demand to be released' – he would say a quiet 'thank you. Is
that all?' and scurry off to his next detainee, like the anxious
White Rabbit always late, late for his appointments in Alice's
Wonderland. His appointments were with detainees in the
other Marshall Square cells – there were sixteen apart from me –
in the Kliptown, Fordsburg, Jeppe, Rosebank, Brixton, and
Rosettenville police stations, where detainees waited in the half-
dark.

At one interview I uttered my usual diatribe against Ninety-Day detention and told the magistrate to tell the Minister it was a sadistic scheme. He wrote with his customary civil-service politeness. He was on his way out when I called over my shoulder 'And tell the Minister I need a bath!' He came back. Was there really no bath? he asked. Only a cold-water tap, I said, and the daily bucket of hot water.

A few days later the Public Works Department arrived. They had instructions to build a shower in the women's section. Builders and planners, paid and amateur, flocked to examine the slope of the floor in the washroom of the large cell, the thickness of the pipes, the outlet to the drain. With great deliberation they argued the best site for the shower and how to cope with its overflow that, if not dammed or run off, would flood the floor of the large cell. Wardresses going off shift reported to their replacements coming on duty the state of the women's shower. In time the cheapest scheme was agreed to by the P.W.D. supervisors. Bricklayer and plasterer moved in with two African labourers and by the end of the day the shower had been screwed in and a small concrete wall, four inches high, had been built to divide the wash-up section from the cell. Pained was on duty and she immediately prophesied disaster.

She was right. A noisy energetic drunk was booked in late that evening. She raged blindly round the cell for some hours, then there was a brief silence: perhaps she was eyeing the bed. I lay in mine waiting for her to settle down. There was the noise of feet shuffling across the floor, then a resounding slap-bump on concrete, then heavy silence. No wardress came until the change of shift the next morning. The drunk woman was found stretched across the low shower wall. Like an obstacle laid across her path it had tripped her at the ankle and caused her to fall headlong into the shower. A doctor was called but he diagnosed nothing more serious than a large head bump. The wall had to go nevertheless; at that rate it would knock out all the drunks as they lurched towards the toilet. The construction of the shower dragged on, the P.W.D. coming back repeatedly to improve the slope of the floor towards the outlet pipe and to put heads together with the wardresses on the perfection of the shower. When finally it ran it gave only cold water, but I used it religiously out of deference to the achievement of the magistrate in reaching the ear of the Minister.

The morning-shift wardress broke her silence.
'Did you hear a shot last evening?' she asked.
I had not.

*

Dennis Brutus, live-wire initiator of the campaign against apartheid in sport, himself sportsman, teacher, impassioned poet, had been shot in the side only two blocks from Marshall Square. He had been taken to Coronation Hospital for an emergency operation. Two policemen in surgical masks stood watch in the operating theatre, police patrolled the hospital grounds and stood guard outside Dennis's ward on the first floor. His doctor, a woman, tried to see him after the operation. The policeman outside the door stopped her. One of them said to the other, 'Shall we arrest her or should I shoot?'

Brutus recovered, despite the complication of pneumonia, and then refused to let the doctors change the dressing on his wound; he demanded to see a representative from the then Federation of Rhodesia and Nyasaland.

Gradually the account was unravelled. Brutus had been in Swaziland at the time that Harold and Arthur had sought temporary refuge there. They had travelled west, by air, to Bechuanaland; Brutus had turned eastwards, had shown his Southern Rhodesian passport at the Swaziland border and had presented himself to the Portuguese authorities of Mozambique, at Mhlumeni near Goba. The passport was valid, the visa freshly issued. The officials were preparing to stamp his passport for a stay of twenty days when the telephone at the border post rang. An inspector was being sent from Lourenço Marques, the capital, to check Brutus's papers, he was told. Four inspectors arrived. Brutus protested that he wanted to return to Swaziland, but he was told he was under arrest. He was taken under escort to Lourenço Marques. A spokesman for the Mozambique Policia Internacional e Defesa Estado (P.I.D.E.) said that the South African Security Branch had been notified of Brutus's arrest.

The Grays dispatched Sergeant Kleingeld and Warrant Officer Halberg to fetch Brutus, who was handed over to them at Komatipoort. The party arrived at Marshall Square as dusk was falling on Tuesday 17 September. As Kleingeld bent to take a suitcase from the boot of the car, Brutus made a dash for it. He sprinted westward, through the peak-hour traffic, chased by Halberg. Kleingeld had fallen and hurt his knee and was out of the chase. Halberg fired and Brutus fell to the pavement outside the Anglo-American building.

An officer of The Grays described Halberg as a 'deadly accurate shot'.

'Four Nations Involved in Row Over Brutus' said a news-paper headline. The manner of his arrest and extradition from Mozambique had led to diplomatic complications which concern South Africa, the Federation, Portugal and Britain, said the report. Brutus had held a valid Rhodesian passport; why had he been handed over to the South African police after entering Mozambique from Swaziland?

South Africa's Minister of External Affairs, Mr Eric Louw, was asked if South Africa had asked Mozambique for Brutus's return. His reply was 'no comment'. Lourenço Marques police headquarters were asked whether Brutus's extradition had been requested by the South African Government. 'We don't know anything about him,' was their reply.

If, it was argued by Brutus's friends, he had been regarded as an undesirable immigrant, normal Portuguese procedure should have been to return him to the country from which he had come (Swaziland), or to the country under whose passport he was travelling (the Federation).

A Federation diplomat called on Brutus in hospital to tell him he could not claim Rhodesian protection or intervention though he had been born in Salisbury and held a Federal passport recently renewed at the Federal diplomatic mission in Pretoria; he had made use of South African nationality, he was told. Brutus's brother, Wilfred J. Brutus, a former merchant seaman, said his brother had never been issued with a South African identity card.

The argument went on for a short while, and then withered beside the fact that Brutus was in the hands of the Security Branch (he had been removed to The Fort in an ambulance), that the Southern Rhodesian Government willingly relinquished any concern with Brutus to South Africa, and Portugal could always be relied on to hand political opponents of the Government over to the police, for South Africa was doing the same for her. The Security Branch patted itself on its back for one of several coups to come involving the capture of political fugitives with the connivance of neighbouring Governments, and the active assistance, in informing, spying and kidnapping, of a white vigilante organization with barely-concealed Government backing.

Brutus was taken to court and charged on four counts with contravention of his banning orders, among them attending a meeting, leaving Johannesburg and leaving the country. Mr Frank Braun, president of the South African Olympic and National Games Association, which was fighting a losing battle to keep colour-bar South African sport in the Olympic Games, gave evidence of how, by unexplained coincidence, detectives had arrived in his office at the moment that Brutus was in the room with members of his committee whom he had come to introduce to a visiting sports journalist. Brutus's lawyer cross-examined the detective who had made the arrest:

Did you know that there would be a meeting on the building on that day?

Yes.

Who told you?

The prosecutor objected to the question.

The magistrate: The objection is sustained. You were asking who the informer was.

Brutus was sentenced to two years' imprisonment with hard labour, which he is serving on Robben Island.

*

I was called out of my cell one morning and I was sure it was for interrogation by the Security Branch. It was a visit by the children, brought by my mother, and arranged at the sympathetic instigation of a non-political neighbour who had tugged at Colonel Klindt's heart-strings by telephone. It did them good to see that I looked the same and talked not of being locked up but of school and the cat, library books, and holidays. Shawn, a vulnerable thirteen-year-old, seemed closest to tears; serious wide-eyed considerate Gillian exerted her usual tight control; and jolly Robyn was diverted throughout the short visit by a conspiracy of her own. They had handed me a fistful of bubblegum on arrival and when the time came to say goodbye, Robyn whispered in between her hugs: 'It's Ch—pp—'s Bubblegum. There are things written on the inside of the paper, something for you to read!'

I chewed the gum and read the wrappings:

'Did you know the skin of an elephant is an inch thick?' 'Did you know the giraffe has seven bones in his neck?' 'Did you know the stars are hundreds of miles apart from each other?' 'Did you know zip fasteners were first used in the nineteenth century?'

'They'll leave you to sweat a while,' a knowledgeable policeman volunteered. They did. For nine days. One morning I heard the approach of the keys to my cell. The wardress appeared. 'They want you,' she said.

Two men were waiting in the small interview room. The taller was Warrant Officer Nel. Lanky, in a drab grey suit, with sandy stringy hair, blue eyes as cold as a fish in an icy bowl, a toneless voice that I never heard utter a spontaneous sound. Sergeant Smit was ginger, an irritable and jerky man. Liverish, it turned out. There was a high deal table and two chairs. The stuffing floated out of the seat of the one so I was offered the second. Nel perched on the edge of the torn seat, and Smit leaned against the wall. This first encounter was hedged in by formal politenesses.

Did I know why I was being detained? Nel asked.

On Living in a Police Station

No, I said.

Patiently he read me the lesson of the day. Clause 17 of the General Law Amendment Act of 1963 states:

Any commissioned officer ... may ... without warrant arrest ... any person whom he suspects upon reasonable grounds of having committed or intending or having intended to commit any offence under the Suppression of Communism Act, 1950 (Act No. 44 of 1950), or under the last-mentioned Act as applied by the Unlawful Organizations Act, 1960 (Act No. 34 of 1960), or the offence of sabotage, or who in his opinion is in possession of any information relating to the commission of any such offence or the intention to commit any such offence, and *detain such person* or cause him to be detained *in custody for interrogation* in connexion with the commission of or intention to commit such offence, *at any place he may think fit, until such person has in the opinion of the Commissioner of the South African Police replied satisfactorily to all questions at the said interrogation, but no such person shall be so detained for more than ninety days on any particular occasion when he is so arrested.*

Was I prepared to answer questions?

I could not possibly know, I said, until I knew what the questions were. But I was being detained to answer questions, Nel repeatedly insisted. Preliminary to prosecution? I asked. Were they preparing a prosecution? How could I answer questions if evidence was being gathered against me? I needed to know what the questions were before I could say if I would answer them.

Like a pet white mouse in a toy ferris wheel, round and round I went. I was bored, I found to my surprise. I had been through this encounter so often, in my imagination, lying in my cell, that I was surprised not to hear them say: 'But you've tried this on us so often before!'

Unexpectedly, Nel took a decision. 'You were a member of the central committee of the Black Hand Secret Society,' he darted at me.

I answered that question – with an incredulous giggle. I was banned from some thirty organizations, over twenty-four of which I had never belonged to anyway. I had heard of a few dozen organizations other than those listed in the usual banning orders. But the whole country knew that the Black Hand Secret Society was an invention of the Security Branch. A reaction question, surely, I made a mental note. I just had time to register the technique when they moved in with a body blow.

'What were you doing at Rivonia?' I filled in my stunned pause with nervous repetitive chatter that I could give no undertaking to answer questions till I knew the full extent of the investigation.

'Why did Joe leave the country?'

'Why did you hold mixed parties?' – 'To mix,' I said.

'What were you doing in South West Africa?'

The questions and the few flippant non-committal fencing replies had become awkward. I felt the producers were noticing that I was missing my cues and not hearing the prompt.

The sergeant had been leaning against the wall. Impatiently he pulled himself erect and said crossly to Nel, 'She thinks she's clever. She's just trying to probe.'

He was right, of course. I knew enough for one interview. The Security Branch knew I had been at Rivonia.

Five days later the two came again. And six days after that. They asked no new questions. Was I prepared to answer questions? Was I prepared to make a statement? A statement on what? Answers to their questions, they said. What questions? I asked. Everything, they said. They wanted to know everything. Secrets. Nel improved on that. 'Top secrets,' he said.

Behind the parrying and the fencing we were baring our teeth at one another.

Yes, I said precipitately, I'll make a statement.

Nel pulled sheets of foolscap from his briefcase and held his pen ready.

I said I could write it myself.

I understand from Warrant Officer Nel, I wrote, that I am being detained in terms of section 17 of Act No. 32 of 1963. (I borrowed his copy of the Government Gazette and wrote out the main drift of the clause.) I could not say if I would answer questions until I knew whether I was being charged with any offence and until I knew the nature of the questions. My verbal formula of evasion filled almost the whole of the foolscap sheet. The two detectives carried this sheet of paper away. They looked relieved, I thought, that this time they had a sheet of paper to take back to headquarters.

On the whole I was visited once a week. Never on the same day of the week twice running, rarely at the same time of the day. The attempts at interrogation seemed desultory. Some sessions were a toneless repetition. 'Are you prepared to make a statement?' – 'How can I?' and I was taken back to my cell. Several times the appearance of the two detectives, or Nel alone, was so brief that I believed it was merely to make the file entry 'Saw Mrs Slovo' as proof that he had checked in for duty.

One week there were two different interrogators.

Swanepoel was squat, bullfrog-like. His face glowed a fiery red that seemed to point to the bottle, but he swore that he had never drunk so it must have been his temper burning through, for Swanepoel's stock-in-trade was his bullying. Higher in rank yet deferring to Swanepoel's belligerence was Van Zyl, a lumbering, large man who tried persuasion in a sing-song oily voice. Van Zyl carried 'Granpa' headache powders in his top pocket; he sometimes offered them to his victims. On Sundays he was a lay preacher, on weekdays he was Swanepoel's interrogation partner. The two of them peddled a mixture of noisy vulgar abuse and suspect avuncular wheedling.

I had sat around for long enough without telling them anything, they said. I had been detained to answer questions. The replies had to be to the satisfaction of the Minister.

How did they know I knew anything? I asked. They knew, they said. I must know. I was 'part of the set-up'.

'The set-up?' I said. 'What set-up?'

My husband, my father, they said. They knew all about *them*. Why did Joe, my husband, leave the country, Swanepoel

53

demanded? He raised his voice. 'He's a coward,' he bellowed. 'He's a coward on the run.'

'Do you really think you can tell me anything about Joe . . .?'

Swanepoel leaned forward. 'And we know he's sent you money from Dar-es-Salaam.' Has he, now? I said. 'Good, it's about time. And why shouldn't he support us?'

'Not money for you,' Swanepoel snarled. 'Money for the movement. . . . We know.'

'You know? Well, if you say so. . . .'

Where did the money come from? the two wanted to know. They kept coming back to this question. Swanepoel blustered and shouted; Van Zyl looked amused when I raised my voice in response. They demanded to know, they insisted I was there to answer questions and answer them I would. 'Surely you know everything already?' I said. 'You keep saying so and look at the bulges in your briefcases, your files must be crammed full.' Their briefcases lay on the table before us. 'Oh, in those we carry our sandwiches and bottles of brandy,' they said. For a moment we were a happy joking family.

Swanepoel tried another tack, then another. He turned to Van Zyl. 'She's too comfortable here. She's having a holiday. We must have her moved to Pretoria. She won't like that.'

Once again he asked why Joe had left the country. 'Joe is no fool,' I said. 'Has it ever struck you that he might have provided for this day? How can you know that I know anything at all? Couldn't he have said to me the day he left, "My dear, when I have gone the chances are that the Security Branch will hold you for ninety days to question you about me . . . so I'm going, but I shan't tell you the reason why. . . . It will be useless for the Security Branch to question you, won't it?"'

Swanepoel's stock-in-trade was to bully and taunt but like most bullies he could not himself stand being teased. His colour rose higher.

'You're an obstinate woman, Mrs Slovo. But remember this. Everyone cracks sooner or later. It's our job to find the cracking point. We'll find yours too.'

On Living in a Police Station

Even now I cannot write how it happened but shortly after this I was given two pieces of information that froze my limbs. First leak: a delegate present at a meeting I had attended at Rivonia with Mandela, Sisulu, and others had blurted information to the police. The Security Branch would have a list of those present at these highly confidential discussions, they would have the agenda items and possibly even an account of what each of us had said. Here was one revealing source of information; were there others? Second leak: the Security Branch was investigating my father and my mother. My father I knew about. Swanepoel had made little attempt to hide his interest in him. Would they act against my mother too? If they had detained James Kantor for being Harold's business associate and brother-in-law, what was to stop them detaining my mother as a lead to my father? The prospect of her detention unnerved me. How would she live in the grime and filth of a cell? The children had lost Joe in June, me at the beginning of August. Judging by the questioning of the Security Branch my father might well be in hiding. I had left the children with heartache but I had the comfort of my mother as substitute. If she was taken, they would be abandoned.

I had to find a way to warn her. I spent a day thinking about how to smuggle out a note, another day composing the message. I got out the sliver of lead hidden in the lining of my suitcase. I wrote the message, but then tore it up. For what if it was intercepted? Instead of forewarning my mother I would be drawing Security Branch fire to her. How write so that an innocent construction could be put on the words? This might be the only message I succeeded in getting through; there was no time to exchange views and debate action, the message had to be blatantly clear. I composed another message, and yet another. Repeating the text of the warning I had received would expose my source of information. Admonishing my mother to caution would be dismissed with impatience. The only way to persuade her to act to safeguard her own freedom, I decided, was to insist, for my sake and theirs, that she take the children away. With infinite trouble I wrote thirty urgent words to send a signal by a laborious procedure that had been devised for a time of extreme need. (I had previously alerted my mother that I would use this way to reach her.) I waited several days to send the signal out, so that it would be picked up as pre-arranged, and then settled down to wait for an acknowledgement. Nothing happened the first day, or the second, the third or fourth. By the fifth I was forced to conclude that the signal had not got through. The transmission system had not worked. If I had needed any fresh reminder here it was: I was insulated against contact and my chances of breaking the isolation even in desperate need were nil.

During my first weeks in the cell I had been impudently buoyant. I was determined to find the stamina to survive this war of attrition. But now I began to feel encumbered by diversionary actions. My parents, and through them the children, were being pulled into the line of fire. What was the Security Branch planning? Who else was on the list to be detained? Who else had turned informer? I lay and worried, before full awakening in the morning, all day, even in my sleep. I was no longer sleeping well.

They have the evidence of the man at the meeting. Whose else? How had they tumbled on Rivonia? The shock of the Thursday afternoon raid a month ago surged back. Kathy had had his hair dyed red, making him look like the cousin of the Portuguese market gardener. Walter Sisulu with straightened hair and Chaplinesque moustache had dispensed with his suits and sported a pullover of vivid design like a sailor's tattoo; he had had toothache that week, and had needed a dentist. (Did they bring him a dentist in his Ninety-Day detention cell?) Govan in blue denim overalls had been dressed like a labourer but had always had a pencil in his hand, writing, drafting, planning. A baker's van had inched along the winding driveway. '*Ons slaan toe!*' [Let's get cracking!] the officer in charge, Lieutenant Van Wyk, had said, and the van had disgorged policemen. Walter had leapt for the window but a police dog had brought him down. Handcuffs had been produced for Raymond, Walter, Govan and Kathy, Rusty and Dennis.

They had taken Arthur and Hazel too. Policemen had played ball with Nicholas and Paul, the two young Goldreich children, and had asked five-year-old Paul for the names of his father's friends. Labourers and domestics on the farm had been rounded up and put into police vans. Each now sat in a solitary cell.

Sequence and incident became jumbled; I found difficulty in disentangling my fears from the facts. I longed for what seemed in retrospect the untroubled emptiness of the early days in detention. I wrestled with decisions that had to be based on the flimsiest shreds of information, my ability to reason bedevilled, I knew, by the lopsidedness that solitary confinement would impose on my reasoning. Did they have enough to convict me? Who else was in detention by now? Who was talking? What was I on record as having said at the Rivonia meeting that had been denounced? I could not remember: meetings at Rivonia tended to merge into one another, and into meetings held elsewhere: there had been many.

I embarked upon a campaign to accommodate myself to the prospect not of ninety days in a cell, but years. The sooner I got used to the idea, I decided, the more easily I would bear it. Once convicted I would be able to read, study, perhaps even write; at worst I could store experiences and impressions for the day I could write. I would struggle to erase self-pity. Hardest of all, I would struggle not to think about the children. They would be elsewhere, where they could grow up without the continuous reminder of me in a prison, and they would have Joe. I had always needed him so-; he would give the children his confidence, his optimism, his humour. It could have been so much worse: Joe might have been sitting in a cell upstairs, and by sheer lucky timing he had got away from the Rivonia raid and the aftermath. I had to stop thinking about the children. I needed all my concentration to handle my own situation ... but of course I couldn't stop thinking about them.

I was called to the interview room. A greying man in a brown suit was pacing impatiently up and down the corridor.

'I'm Colonel Klindt,' he said. 'I came to tell you that **your** mother was due to visit you today but she telephoned this morning to say that she would not be able to come. She's ill, but it's nothing serious, a stomach upset. You shouldn't worry, I understand there's a lot of it about.'

Colonel Klindt, the head of the largest Security Branch organization in the country, come personally to tell me that my mother was out of sorts . . .

'My men tell me you're not answering questions,' he said. 'Is that right?'

'How can I answer questions . . .?' I reached for my patter. 'I can't say that I will answer questions until I know if I'm to be prosecuted . . .'

'You're going to be prosecuted,' Colonel Klindt said.

'Alone, or with others?' I asked.

'With others.'

My mother was granted a visit. Colonel Klindt came to the prisons rarely, I gathered. For the most part he sat in his office in The Grays supervising his squads of detective-interrogators, going in person on very important raids . . . and making himself available, when he was so inclined, to the anxious relatives of detainees. He dispensed visits entirely at his discretion. My mother danced attendance at The Grays with powers of attorney, letters from the bank, forms needing my signature. She was granted one request out of ten.

This time she said, 'Do you want to hear all the news, or just the good news?'

'All the news, bad news too.'

'Ronnie's been detained,' she said. 'I'd rather they had taken me.'

Ronnie is my brother.

Pained fetched me out for exercise. Twice while I walked up and down the yard she had the heavy door opened and put her head through to peer at me. The second time she called in the cell warder and said in my hearing, 'She's got a suitcase to pack. We'd better tell her now.'

'Tell me what?' I demanded.

'Mr Nel said we had to get you ready. He's coming to fetch you.'

An hour later Nel came, with a new detective, Van Rensburg, who, I discovered, had detained my brother and was in charge of his case, and a woman clerk from the C.I.D. offices who was released from her typewriter for the morning to act as escort.

The car was driven in the direction of Pretoria. Why, I asked Nel, why was I being taken to Pretoria?

'A more permanent home for you, Mrs Slovo,' he said.

Chapter Three

ISOLATION IN A VACUUM

The car was a two-door sedan and I was put in the back with the escort. Nel drove and Van Rensburg swivelled round to ask me a question.

'Where's your father?'

'You lock me up for two months and ask me that? How could I possibly know?'

'Think hard and you'll probably have a good idea ... your woman's intuition. ...'

I had no intuition, I said.

He wouldn't like to be locked up under Ninety Days, Van Rensburg said. He didn't mind telling me that what he would miss most would be books.

'Really!' I said. 'What books do you read?'

'Philosophy,' he said.

At the outskirts of Pretoria the car turned left into a road signposted 'Department of Prisons'. One piece of prison architecture followed another: double storeys in concrete with fake castellations and imitation towers, huge iron-studded doors with smaller doors in them.

The detectives didn't seem to know their way. Perhaps, like me, they were visiting the Women's Central Prison for the first time.

In the Matron's office a bird chirped in a cage on a pedestal and an irritable-looking Pekingese with tiny teeth bared in blackish gums lay on the carpet. The windows looked out on to a bed of snapdragons. 'Ah, what the hand of a woman can do,' the two detectives cooed ingratiatingly. Nel, Van Rensburg, and the Matron put their heads together and repeated after one another the instructions in Afrikaans about what to do with me. No visitors whatsoever. No books. No contact with anyone of whatever kind.

'I've got a lovely room waiting for her,' the Matron said.

Isolation in a Vacuum

She looked to the doorway where a row of wardresses in khaki skirts, starched pink shirts and khaki forage caps perched on stiff lacquered hair had formed. They stiffened to attention and the entire row rushed forward and ranged itself about me when the Matron indicated that I should be escorted upstairs. 'Not all of you!' the Matron ordered, and three of the wardresses disentangled themselves from the body of eight and ushered me to the stairs. I minced in my high heels and thrust my bosom out firmly in my charcoal suit, free to impress them, I thought, while I was still outside a cell. I was so preoccupied with making a dignified exit that I dropped the biscuit tin I was carrying and had to get down on hands and knees to scoop up the biscuit pieces.

The 'nice room' was at the head of the stairs. It was two-and-a-half times the size of my Marshall Square cell, as bright as the previous cell had been gloomy. The bed had sheets. One barred window high in the wall overlooked the front of the prison; a second was an excellent vantage-point from which to view the staircase. The cell had double doors: one was solid steel with a peephole in the centre; the inner one was of mesh and bars at two-inch intervals. The wardresses carried in an enamel water jug, a china cup and saucer and plate, a fork and a spoon, and a gleaming white table-cloth. My housekeeper instincts surged and I arranged these acquisitions in tidy rows, hung my jacket from the bars of the stair window, and placed my shoes under the bed.

I would have an hour a day for exercise and could take my bath then, the Matron said. Couldn't I bathe in the morning? I pleaded and the Matron conceded. I asked when I would be let out to the toilet. She looked at me in astonishment. 'But you've got the po,' she said, and pulled from under the bed a large enamel bucket with lid. I couldn't possibly use that, I said. I couldn't and I would not. She pressed me for a reason but I persisted stubbornly without giving a reason and, afraid perhaps that I was reticent about divulging some intimate detail of my personal hygiene, she conceded again. I would be let out to bath in the morning, for an hour of exercise at midday, and briefly before lock-up time in the late afternoon to go to the toilet block. For the rest of the time I would remain in my cell.

The wardresses withdrew, pulling the two heavy doors behind them, and the noise subsided to the ground floor below me. I rushed to the peephole but it looked on to a blank wall. I was blinkered like a horse. Only when I was taken out of my cell three times each day could I steal hurried glances to left and right of me as I was hustled up and down the stairs. This was the only time I could see my surroundings on the first floor. There were two endless parallel corridors on each side of my centred cell, each corridor lined with rows of standardized barred cells, bank safety deposit boxes for humans. But no sound came from these cells. Only the one nearest me seemed to be occupied. A high stool stood in front of this cell which was closed only with the inner bar-and-mesh door. All day and all through the electrically lighted night a wardress perched silently on the stool. Inside the cell an African woman sat at a table. Her head was bare and lowered on her propped elbows. I could not see her face. I never saw her look up or heard her speak. Four days in succession I asked the wardresses why she was guarded day and night. They never replied; they were under orders not to speak to me. On the fifth day she had been moved. I don't know where they took her. I had suspected all along, and now it seemed confirmed, that she had been a condemned prisoner in the condemned cell.

When she was taken away I had the floor all to myself. My cell was the posh front room of the house. It might indeed have passed for a room, not a cell, if not for the bars on the windows and the doors which propagated themselves by twilight and by night with the play of light on walls and ceiling.

The window on the stairs was unrewarding as a look-out post. Except when wardresses came to bring me food or fetch me out, the staircase was unused. I remained alone in my prison eyrie, brooding over the activity that echoed from far parts of the building.

To see through the larger window I had to stand on tiptoe on the iron bedhead and hang from the bars of my cage. Immediately under the window was the main road of the Prison Department estate and across the way – mocking my incarceration – stretched a splendid swimming-pool, complete with high diving-board and trampoline, lawns and flower gardens, and, farther afield but still well within my view, two bowling-greens and several tennis courts. These were the recreation grounds of the (white) Prisons Department staff and their families. From the barred window I watched week-end goings-on with curiosity that soon soured to resentment. Warders in khaki uniform would go through the turnstile at the entrance to emerge at the edge of the gleaming pool as the bronzed muscled young men of the airline travel posters that advertise Sunny South Africa. Their girl-friends wore bikinis and carried Italian straw bags. The couples sunbathed and swam, dived and splashed, lazed and flirted. It was as normal a scene as anywhere on a South African week-end and the very normality was a rankling affront to me. I found myself watching the arrival of every sporting warder and wardress to see if they would raise their eyes to the barred windows opposite. No one ever did.

I hung from the bars for hours at a time. All week gangs of African convicts laboured in preparation for the week-ends, sweeping, hosing, planting, weeding, rolling the grass, and trimming its edges to nail-scissor-clipped neatness. Armed guards stood duty over them as they worked at the bent, half-running jog which seems to be required prison posture and pace for African men. They wore dirty off-white singlets and shorts and were shoeless. Lean to the bone, they were animated stick figures, incongruously subservient to the watching, armed guards in such carefree surroundings. By the week-ends the convicts had been herded back into their jail; their labour was done and the water and the lawns lay invitingly at the feet of their guards. The more distant bowling-greens seemed the preserve of the senior prison staff and their portly figures and slow rolling gait told of greater dignity and heavier responsibility.

I encountered, close-up, only two members of the senior

prison staff: the Prison Commandant, Colonel Au'camp, and his second-in-command, Major Bowen.

On the second day of my stay in Pretoria my door was flung open to reveal the colonel. I did not know that prison regulations demand that every prisoner must stand to ramrod attention every time a wardress, let alone the chief, appeared. I had been lying on the bed and the Matron was aghast. Even she stood up for her colonel, she reproved me later. I reminded her that she had voluntarily enlisted in the force; I had not. After that reproof, though my stance would not have passed muster on any parade, I did rise to my feet whenever the Matron or one of her superiors came to the cell. Colonel Au'camp seemed wary of coming in. He stood in the doorway and looked hard at me with small, pig-like eyes in a fleshy face, the faintest suggestion of a smirk on his mouth. On the second day his smirk was a little wider and I decided that he was warming to the idea of having a woman Ninety-Dayer in the clutches of his jail. By contrast Major Bowen was a demonstrative, garrulous man. On his inspection days he marched right into the cell and moved his swagger stick up and down in time to his query: 'Well? How's things? This is a prison and we are bound by regulations but if there is anything we can do to make your stay pleasant, you can tell us.' Major Bowen was exceeding himself as a host, but by his query to the Matron accompanying him on the inspection we both understood that he knew nothing about the conditions of Ninety-Day detention. 'Have you told her she can have her family to visit?' he asked, probably thinking that as I was dressed in my own clothes I must be an awaiting-trial prisoner. 'Oh no!' the Matron said. 'She can't see anyone. The Security Branch said so.' Between us we conveyed to the major that I could see no one, was given no work to do, had nothing but the Bible to read. He was readily sympathetic. Nothing to read, he said, '*Dis swaar*' [That's hard] and then, encouragingly to me. 'You'll make the best of it. Read the Book. And get down on your knees, down on your knees.'

I read the Book, from the first page to the last, first the Old

Testament, then the New. When I reached the last page I started again with the first. I memorized psalms and proverbs:

> A fool's mouth is his destruction
> And his lips are the snare of his soul

and

> Confidence in an unfaithful man in time of trouble
> Is like a broken tooth, and a foot out of joint

memorizing and storing up references to my predicament at the hands of informers and the Security Branch.

I revelled in the energy of the Creation and the narration of the exile, in the tumultuous Revelations; I skipped with impatience through the elaborate collection of taboo and ritual, the wearisome census reports of the Book of Numbers, the bewildering time-sequences of the Chronicles. I felt close to the melancholy of Jeremiah and Lamentations. I wondered how comfort could be found, by those who use the Book for refuge, in the baleful and avenging God of the Old Testament. The Gospels revealed a new divinity: compassionate and man-size. But then along came Paul with his rabbinical training to out-argue points of doctrine with the most astute dogmatists of the older school, to advocate submission to earthly rulers and non-involvement in questions of the righteousness of kingdoms on earth.

I had been reading the Bible steadily for two months in Marshall Square and there were days – for all the lurid visions and attractive prophecies of disaster – when I could not bring myself to open the covers. Given commentaries I might have advanced to a more profound examination of the Gospels and Paul's sermons and letters but the Security Branch conceded us the Bible not to deepen our faith and understanding and improve our religious erudition, but out of deference to the Calvinist religion of the Cabinet and the Nationalist Party which, mysteriously, justifies apartheid policy by its interpretation of divine teaching, and could therefore deny the ballast of this theology to no prisoner, not even an atheist political.

Giving us the Bible, they seemed to think, fulfilled the State's Christian duty to us as prisoners. We had the Book and our consciences in solitude; the interrogation methods of the Security Branch would, it was hoped, do the rest.

I stayed in the cell for all but ninety-five minutes each day. But I stuck to my resolve never to use the po. I hung on till the day shift took over from the night shift at about seven o'clock in the mornings and freed me from my cell to lock me in the bathroom block for thirty minutes. At midday I was fetched once again and locked in the exercise yard for an hour. Lock-up time was at half past four, and about twenty minutes before the day shift left the prison I was let out for a few minutes. This was the usual routine but it was disrupted on Sundays and on prison holidays. In the second week after my transfer to Pretoria lock-up time was inexplicably brought forward to two o'clock and I remained locked in for a stretch of seventeen hours, still without using the po. My bladder passed the jail endurance test as well if not better than any other part of me.

The day began with a hooter blast at seven o'clock and a great din from down below. I could not tell what was happening except by the bedlam clatter of tin plates and the shouting of orders by the wardresses. I imagined the communal cells being opened to let prisoners out for their platefuls of cold caked porridge, the standard prison fare in the morning. By the time it was my turn to be let out there were no prisoners to be seen, only giant trolleys on which the food must have been brought from the kitchen. Two wardresses – whenever I was escorted anywhere it was by two wardresses, a walking sentinel on each side of me – trotted me off to the bathhouse, and when I was locked inside, the sick parade of the prisoners was called. This was my chance to see some of the inmates of the jail. There was generally a delay while the wardresses went to await the arrival of the doctor, so I moved to the bathroom window to gaze at the African women.

They wore coffee-brown wrap-around overalls and bright red *doeks*, and, under their brown skirts, short petticoats of striped white and blue flannel. Several of the women had young babies on their backs. Tied to their skirts were mugs and spoons. When there were no guards standing over them they relaxed in their own company and talked and laughed together. Several of them would generally catch sight of me staring at them through the grille of the bathroom and point me out to the others, and we would make gestures to one another across the yard.

Very soon the doctor would be ushered up the stairs into the room that served as a clinic and he would go through the sick queue like a dose of salts; judging by the rate of his progress he was doing little more than dispense doses of salts.

I would be left in the bathhouse for thirty minutes, then my two guards would reappear and escort me back upstairs.

By chance one day I caught sight of two white women in prison garb standing at the door of the hospital. They were subdued creatures with drab hair and timid movements. They must have been in this prison pending transfer to one of the women's jails like Ermelo, Nylstroom, or Pietersburg, for Pretoria Central was reserved for African women serving terms of six months or longer.

The gestures through the window between the African women and me were the only contact for the day with anyone apart from the prison staff. Back in my cell I would eat my breakfast as slowly as I could, trying to prolong the operation, but somehow I could never get it to last longer than twenty-five minutes. Then I had to pass the time of four and a half hours till my exercise period.

By midday, when I was taken out, the yard was deserted (the African prisoners were locked in their cells for their midday meal) except for rows and rows of washing hanging everywhere, on washing lines and the split pole fence round the yard, and covering the grass. The prison had become a laundry. I did a painstaking scrutiny of every item of washing, as though it had been laid out for my inspection. The fence was draped with rough mailbags. Everywhere I looked were office towels marked S.A.P. – South African Police – which must have been collected from the police stations. The prize exhibits hung from the lines. There was every conceivable article of clothing, mostly in good condition. Each item was marked with a number and a well-known Afrikaans name. I wandered between rows of dresses, shirts, vests, blouses, shorts, and jeans marked Van der Merwe, Kemp, Prinsloo, Erasmus, Van Wyk, Buitenkamp, Rossouw, Potgieter, Coetzee, Van Zyl, and Du Plessis. On the last line three large pairs of aertex underpants with nifty American-type press studs hung side by side. They were marked P. K. Le Roux. P. K. Le Roux is South Africa's Minister of Agriculture. Suddenly the shot went home. The prisoners were earning the jail's keep by taking in the washing of Cabinet Ministers, important civil servants, and well-to-do Pretoria families who were having a good laundry job done cheaply and were at the same time aiding the rehabilitation of the country's reprobates. The women scrubbed for their sins the sheets of the Director of Prisons and the hand-towels of the myriads of civil servants who stamped, cancelled, and countermanded their passes and their permission to remain in the city; and I took my exercise amidst the underpants of the Minister of Agriculture.

I meandered round the yard, picking my way through the washing laid on the grass, balancing on one foot on the low polished walls round the flower-beds. Everything that could take a surface of polish was rubbed up daily: the paving-stones, the large flower-pots, the window-sills, the drains. The place was as neat as a box of pins and only a steady hum from the ground floor cells disturbed the lunch-hour quiet. Except for the day that blood-chilling screams came from a little brick building in the farthest corner of the yard. The building was labelled *Isolasie – Isolation* and was the punishment block. The screams began in a low register at regular intervals, then mounted steadily in shrillness and frenzy to become a horrifyingly demented human siren with a noise volition of its own. Five wardresses moved in a body to the isolation block. They emerged a few minutes later. I don't know what they said or did to the inmate, but the howling stopped. One of my two walking sentinels come to take me back to the cell that day was the

Matron. I asked about the howling. 'This is a prison, you know,' she said.

The Matron was an old-timer in the service. Like the others 'long at this game' (her words) she was approachable, at times even sympathetic. She must have been thirty years older and thirty years longer in the service than the oldest member of her staff, and she was due for retirement in a few years. Her pre-Nationalist Government vintage was fast being replaced in the prison service with staffs who accept apartheid wholeheartedly and judge wrongdoers by apartheid lights : they despise all non-whites as inferiors bound, sooner or later, to land in prison; and they are contemptuous of the whites in jails as malicious or failing creatures who have let their (white, superior) side down.

The wardresses were semi-educated teenagers; in South Africa girls and youths can enter the prison service at the tender age of sixteen. Prison service seems to run in families and many a policeman's daughter becomes a wardress to keep the service in the family. The young wardresses came on duty primping their hair and chattering to their fellow-wardresses about the previous night out with their boy-friends; when the hooter blew they rushed off pulling straight their stocking seams and impatient to take up with their boy-friends where they had left off the night before. They were incurious, uninterested creatures, callous not by deliberation but by an utter lack of responsiveness except on the most superficial level. They were unseeing, unfeeling, uncaring keepers of the hundreds of women whose daily lives they ran.

Yet the young girls in uniform were less frightening than the prison graduates who fill the higher ranks in the service and become assistant-matrons and matrons. These superior creatures are promoted to supervisory posts after they have emerged from courses laid on for the Department of Prisons by the University of Pretoria. The prison graduates hold certificates for their prowess in the theory of subjects like criminal psychology and penology. The youngsters are ignorant and insensitive; the intellectual prison viragos are high-handed, opinionated and inflexible : their innate prejudices against the African, the poor and the socially maladjusted have been moulded into doctrine by glib lectures on criminal types.

South Africa is in the throes of penal reform. To this end certain improvements, mainly for whites, in uniform, food, and privileges, have been introduced; but basically the prisons cling to the idea that their function is not reform and rehabilitation but vengeance. The accent is on punishment, the harsher the better; longer and longer sentences; less freedom; higher walls; thicker bars. The prisoner is locked in, his horizon shrunk to the area bound by the bars of his cell; he is left to do labouring routine for most of the week and contemplate his sins for the rest. The prisons are judged by their state of cleanliness, not by the responsiveness of the prisoners to rehabilitation, or by good relations between prisoners and prison staff, for of these there is nothing to see. '*Netjies*' [neat, or tidy] was the word the Matron most liked to use, and when she came round her gaze inevitably went first to the state of the bed. Hence the regulation, relaxed in my case, that no prisoner should use the bed between rising and lock-up time in the late afternoon. I could not easily read the Bible by the electric light because the bulb was obscured by a protective mesh basket; the cover could not be left hanging ajar regardless of what the dim covered light was doing to my eyesight because it would not look '*netjies*'.

During the day the noises of the prison moved from the building in which I was locked to the laundries and the drying yards, but at night the prisoners, the guards, and a turbulent crowd of sounds returned. For an hour or two before the jail settled down for the night, the night-shift wardresses' voices were stridently abusive. When there was a clamour from a cell the wardresses would bang on the outside of the door with their fists and yell insults and vulgarities by way of rebuke for the noise. They called the African women '*swart slange*', '*kaffermeide*', '*swartgat*', '*aap*', and '*swartgoed*' [Black snakes, kaffir-girls, black holes, apes, and black rubbish], and the swearing seemed to reassure them of their elevation in authority over the inferior and the delinquent. But the noise did not last long and the stretch of night slid into quiet and loneliness for me, and overcrowding in the foetid stench of the downstairs cells for the African women who slept beside open sanitary buckets during the night.

I was in Pretoria Central Prison for twenty-eight days. It was like being sealed in a sterile tank of glass in a defunct aquarium. People came to look at me every now and then and left a ration of food. I could see out of my glass case and the view was sharp and clear, but I could establish no identity with what I could see outside, no reciprocal relationship with anyone who hove in view. In Marshall Square my sooty surroundings and the general air of gloom about the old police station would have justified melancholy, but I had been buoyant and refractory. Pretoria shone of bright polished steel and I grew increasingly subdued. My imprisonment was an abandonment in protracted time. I reflected on the new-found skill of the Security Branch in subjecting people to an enforced separation, a dissociation, from humanity. I felt alien and excluded from the little activity I saw about me; I was bereft of human contact and exchange. What was going on in the outside world? No echoes reached me. I was suspended in limbo, unknowing, unreached.

I read the Bible, day-dreamed, tried to shake myself into disciplined thinking. I devised a plot for a novel. The characters were me and my friends, all cast in heroic mould. We planned and organized in opposition to the Government, called for strikes and acts of civil disobedience, were harassed and chivvied by the police, banned, and arrested. Then we were locked in prison cells and here I was again, grappling with life in a cell. I did better than that. I spent hours getting behind the political declarations of my characters, dissecting their private inclinations, scrutinizing their love affairs and marriages, their disillusionments and idle talk. When my imagination faltered I turned again to the Bible. I was ravenous for reading matter. One day during the early part of my stay in Pretoria I was in the yard during exercise hour and saw a scrap of paper in the dustbin for cinders from the kitchen high combustion stoves. I fished it out and held it between my thumb and forefinger to devour the words. It was a prison card and recorded prisoner's name, number, crime, and sentence. Perhaps a dozen words in all but to me they were like an archaeological find, proof that some people in this society recognized the value of written language and were able to use it. Even better than this find was the ration of brown sugar that started to arrive every few days, for the six or eight ounces were rolled in a cone of paper, printed paper, torn from old magazines. This way I feasted on a few torn paragraphs from the *War Cry*, organ of the Salvation Army, and once only, tantalizingly, I got a short jagged piece from the *Saturday Evening Post*. Around this extract I tried to improvise a version of a serial *à la* James Bond in which all the action centred round a jail break from Pretoria Central – my cell. Generally, though, my sugar ration was wrapped in an advertisement.

Unlike the Zweig character in *The Royal Game*, I chanced upon no chess manual in a visit to Gestapo headquarters and even if I had I doubt if I could have summoned the powers of concentration to learn the game without board or pieces. I played child-like games in my head: going through the letters of the alphabet for names of writers, composers, scientists, countries, cities, animals, fruit, flowers, and vegetables. As the days went on I seemed to grow less, not more proficient at this game. This was the time I should have been able to feed on the fat of my memory, but I had always had a bad memory (the Security Branch did not believe that one!) and had relied all my life on pencil, notebook, Press clipping, the marking in the margin of a book to recall a source, a fact, a reference. Poetry that I had learned at school fled from me; French verbs were elusive. I lived again through things that had happened to me in the past: conversations and involvements with people, glowing again at a few successes, recoiling with embarrassment at frequent awkwardnesses. I put myself through a concentrated self-scrutiny but in a scattered, disorganized fashion and I found myself not with a clearer insight into myself in this abnormal situation, but with a diffused world of the past diverting me from the poverty of the present. I was appalled at the absence of my inventive and imaginative powers. But I determined to survive by adjusting to a state of enforced hibernation. This was life at quarter-pace. It was a matter of waiting for time to go by, a matter of enduring, an anaesthetizing of self to diminish problems and defeat the dragging passage of days. Life in suspension was the perfect trap for a meandering mind like mine. Day-dreams replaced activity and purposeful thinking. Partly it was confinement in a vacuum that was doing this to me, but it was partly a succumbing to my own nature and to the difficulty, which I felt acutely, of thinking and composing systematically without the aid of pencil and paper.

The routine activities I could organize for myself were few, and, however I struggled to stretch them out, they were over disappointingly soon and I had to sink back again into inertia. I made the bed carefully several times a day, I folded and re-folded my clothes, re-packed my suitcase, dusted and polished everything in sight, cleaned the walls with a tissue. I filed my nails painstakingly. I plucked my eyebrows, then the hair from my legs, one hair at a time, with my small set of tweezers. (When I got into the sun I pulled out the strands of grey hair growing at my temples.) I unpicked seams in the pillow-slip, the towel, the hem of my dressing-gown, and then, using my smuggled needle and thread, sewed them up again, only to un-pick once more, and sew again. The repetition of these meaningless tasks and the long loneliness made me a prisoner of routines and I found myself becoming obsessional, on the constant lookout for omens. I listened for the sound of motor-car tyres on the gravel road outside the window, tried to guess the make of the car, and then climbed to my observation post to check and to give myself black marks if I were wrong. I found myself arranging bets with myself on the day of the week the Security Branch would call; whether it would be the colonel or the major on inspection duty; whether it would take me ten or fifteen seconds to suck in my breath and then dive under the cold shower in the mornings. I threw pips into a paper bag I used as a waste-paper basket; if I missed Vorster was winning, if I hit target three times in succession I would be released at the expiry of the first ninety days.

Ninety days. I calculated the date repeatedly, did not trust my calculation, and did it all again. Every day I repeated that little rhyme 'Thirty days hath September' and I counted days from 9 August, the date of my arrest. My wall calendar had been left behind at Marshall Square; in Pretoria my calendar was behind the lapel of my dressing-gown. Here, with my needle and thread, I stitched one stroke for each day passed. I sewed seven upright strokes, then a horizontal stitch through them to mark a week. Every now and then I would examine the stitching and decide that the sewing was not neat enough and the strokes could be more deadly exact in size; I'd pull the thread out and re-make the calendar from the beginning. This gave me a feeling that I was pushing time on, creating days, weeks, and even months. Sometimes I surprised myself and did not sew a stitch at the end of the day. I would wait three days and then give myself a wonderful thrill knocking three days off the ninety.

Minutes, hours, days, weeks are measurements of time for normal living. For the prisoner in idle isolation, hours and days go by too slowly for them to be acceptable measurements of time. Rather, I decided, measure time as the period of musing before and after a meal, before and after a stretch of sleep, before and after exercise, before and after an interrogation.

I still had my watch. I glued my eyes to the small hand and tried to *see* the passage of time. Surely if I looked hard enough, unblinking, I would see the minute hand move? If I could see time passing it would travel faster, surely. I glared at the hand; it moved as I stared at it, but I did not see the movement.

I riveted my eyes to the window trying to make time pass in the activities of others but I was conscious all the while of what I was trying to do and time, I now learned, did not move while you watched it. Like sand dribbling through an hour-glass the passage of time became a physical act dribbling through my consciousness. It seemed I had to push time on for it to move at all, for in my cell it had lost its own momentum.

While time was passing it crawled. Yet when it had passed it had flown out of all remembrance. When I thought back I could not recall how previous days had passed, or what I had done in the weeks gone by in Marshall Square and Pretoria. There was so little to distinguish one day from the other. Feeling, experience, accumulated, but without relation to days or nights or artificial markings of time. The stitches behind the dressing-gown lapel were certificates of endurance. What I had endured now became rapidly buried in part oblivion, like any unpleasant and humiliating experience.

It was not only the pain of existing in a vacuum. It was the indefiniteness of it all. As the Security Branch detectives said at every possible opening: 'This is the first period of ninety days; there can be another after that, and yet another.' I was convinced that everyone, myself included, could make an adjustment to a known situation. Unknown numbers, many of them in South Africa my closest friends, are living through prolonged prison terms, splendidly adaptable. But the greater part of this matter of adjustment is knowing to what to adjust. Deadly boredom can be withstood if there is an end in sight. A prisoner, even one facing a life term, has some security in the cessation of fear of the unknown.

The Security Branch had devised a situation in which its victim was plagued with uncertainty, apprehension, and aloneness; every day that passed in a state of active anxiety about the outcome of the incarceration and the purpose of the interrogation sessions stripped the prisoner of the calm, the judgement, and the balance which were required equipment to cope with continued isolation and the increased strain of interrogation sessions.

Yet, I told myself, I was subjected to no beating, no physical pain. The passage of time in anxiety was painful, and my ulcer was the recording instrument of that discomfort. But theoretically one could endure for years like this, in cold storage, with the pulse reduced. I was determined to endure the first spell of ninety days, and then make a further adjustment to whatever came after that. It would be ignominious to be defeated by enforced solitude and those inept boorish inquisitors of the Nationalists. Any weakening to them would be a waste of the unending days spent holding out against them. I would accommodate myself to life in the Pretoria cell as I had done in Marshall Square.

Others were having to do the same. The cells all about me stood empty, but for each vacant cell near mine there was one somewhere else in a South African jail or police station filled by a Ninety-Dayer. We were all serving time.

As the days went by I hauled myself up to the window overlooking the swimming-bath less frequently. I did not belong to that company outside; I now actively resented it; it was oblivious of me and those like me. But every now and then as I hung from this observation post, part of my world came into view, and then my spirits soared.

W. got out of a car. She was carrying a basket. This must be the day she took laundered clothes and food to Y., sitting a mile away in Pretoria's Local Jail, and on her day's prison round she was doing stint for my mother by bringing food for me. Y., W. always said, was contemptuous of people who sat in jail doing nothing. He had organized himself a stub of pencil, kept a diary in the form of letters to W., and miraculously smuggled them out to her.

*

. . . about myself here. My cell is approximately ten by eight. It has a table and a hard wooden stool, backless. In one corner is a raised platform on which is enthroned the sanitary pot so-called. That is all. There is a square window about eight to nine feet up, barred with wire-mesh over glass that is so heavily crusted in dust that you really see through a glass darkly. Through it I can see the sky and just the tip of a brick gable of the jail hospital. Blankets and the felt mat on which we sleep must be kept rolled and folded against the table from 6 a.m. to supper. Clothes, food, toilet articles are either neatly laid out on the table or kept in paper carrier bags. For some reason known only to the obscure civil-service mind, no suitcases or bags of any sort are allowed, only

Isolation in a Vacuum

paper carrier bags or topless cardboard boxes. At supper-time shoes must be placed outside cell doors, for some equally obscure reason, and must remain there until breakfast. The light is recessed into the wall behind wire mesh so as to throw a beam of light across the cell and leave everything below four feet in shadow.

I am finding the nights worse than the days. Lights out at 8 p.m. I try to find exercises to keep me up till 8.30. But then I wake too early and from dawn to 5.30 is spent turning and tossing having fearful nightmare dreams. Quite awful and I contemplate getting up and pacing. But no shoes! So I just stay and suffer. I recounted to myself memories of childhood, not in full but to try to discover what makes a man face trial for treason twice in a matter of seven years.

I pace my cell, for two hours I reckon, thinking about the silly tedious time-consuming and primitive jobs I have done at one time or another, and seen done, and then invent ways of doing them. There are a few good ones; there may even be gold in them.

Incredible how fertile one's ingenuity becomes when there is all the time in the world to exercise it, no distractions or stimuli at all.

I have been keeping a record and find that I am averaging eighteen words (spoken) a day. 'Thank you' three times for meals. 'May I have a match, please?' twice at exercise times.

I keep my vocal chords exercised with an evening song session, taking advantage of the captive audience, B., H., and two warders outside, and the quite remarkable bathroom-type acoustics of the cell which enable me to go from basso profondo to mezzosoprano! Aided of course by the fact that I've cut this smoking jazz down to two a day for the second thirty days and intend to drop it entirely for the third. Just one of the gimmicks I'm trying out to ensure that I stay strictly non-obsessional and as non-neurotic as possible in circumstances specially designed for creating neuroses.

We exercise in a dreary enclosed yard, slate floor, cells all round three sides, open shower, w.c.s, tap in centre. We are not allowed to talk. We pace up and down not talking, really rather grim.

There is sun on one side so we stick to the narrow sunny strip.

One Hundred and Seventeen Days

When we first got here we could only just get our heads into the sun by hugging the wall. Since the search which now appears to have been inspired by the finding of a note from one of us in —'s Bible – silly clot – vigilance is at its height and even muttering in the yard is very difficult.

If you could only see the searches now, they get more and more serious like the F.B.I. looking for atomic secrets. Partly the reason is that they know there is a pen somewhere and they suspect B. or me; partly it is that this has become a personal matter in which the warder seems to think his standing is at stake if he does not succeed in tracking it down.

I am unable to think of the torments the children must be having at school. Other kids can be such monsters over things they do not understand . . .

My nerves are still pretty jumpy but much better than the awful period of sixty/seventy days when I really thought I would not be able to see this through. Ten days ago, especially at breakfast-time, I used to sit on my stool so utterly broken and beaten that it took me all my strength to get myself to stand up and face another day. I feel easier, less tense . . . but sleep less, wake earlier and pace the floor more and more. Most days I am up and pacing half an hour or more before the 5.30 bell and lights go on. And today, for instance, have been pacing almost all day except for time at writing. But still, relatively slow, controlled pacing, not the frenzied speed-gathering pacing of my worst days. . . . I know I am pretty close to the end of my nervous tether. I am at my worst at breakfast and a few hours thereafter, then pick up during the day. The prospect is really bleak – unless I am charged, which is what I hope for. Just to be able to talk to people!

The prospect of another ninety days fills me with such awful depression and fear that I cannot bear to contemplate it.

Am very fluttery internally, for no special reason, and feel as though I am as old as Father Time, and shaky as a leaf . . .

It is hell, not just the aloneness and solitude of tedium, but the devilish neurotic fears, anxieties, and tensions that can work up with only one's mind for company and nothing to move it to think except one's own troubles. You can't imagine what this does to you. You become not just the centre but the whole of your universe, your own fate, your own future. Nothing you do or say can possibly affect the life of anyone else, or so it seems.

What little courage I have gradually erodes in loneliness with no one near to sustain me.

Nothing has given me worse torment than the fear that something will happen to you or that you may be dragged into this nightmare situation. This tortures me almost to distraction. On days when I expect you I age a year with every hour that passes. I keep telling myself this is madness, as it is, but reasoning does not help against unreasonable fear.

I am not a very brave man, and it is the fear of the imagination rather than the real threats that I am not fit to stand.

This life is having its effect. I find that with many technical problems, for example inventing, my mind is so completely empty of all else that it operates with what seems to me magical clarity. (Is this itself a sign of madness?) But on questions which involve value judgements, emotional assessments, I am hopelessly out of control. I no longer really trust my judgement as distinct from my thinking. . . .

Does Esmé know that Dennis is in chains? Both ankles joined by a long clanging chain, day and night, which is standard treatment for escapees. I think the day he was brought back here I nearly wept. This is really the saddest sight I have ever seen, really the saddest sight ever. . . .

Esmé did know that Dennis was in chains. S. had come to see Hilda. 'I've been doing Dennis's washing,' *she said (Esmé was a thousand miles away in Cape Town with the two Goldberg children, trying to earn an income that would keep the family during the long term of the trial when the Rivonia men would emerge from solitary confinement into open court).* 'When I collected his clothes yesterday they were torn and blood-stained . . . I'm terribly disturbed. What do you think has happened to Dennis?' *The two women inspected the clothing. There were blood-stains on the trousers and two huge tears in the back of the jacket. The women thought that only police dogs could have ripped the cloth.*

(They were not to know until later that Dennis had ripped the holes himself and had used the jacket over his face and neck to protect himself from the jagged glass on the top of the fourteen-foot-high prison wall he had scaled in his escape attempt.) Dennis, the women knew, was no longer in Pretoria. He had been moved to Vereeniging Prison, and the alarm of the women grew when they realized that the food parcels they were leaving for Dennis at The Grays lay untouched for days. There was nothing for it but to urge Esmé to come north to press the Security Branch for news of her husband. Colonel Klindt was abrupt and uninterested until Esmé held up the gashed and blood-stained clothing. Then he told Esmé about Dennis's escape attempt over an impossibly high wall and how he had been caught by some mischance at just about the last wall or barrier. Esmé was granted a visit to Dennis. She saw him, in chains, but cheerful. He asked about the children and told Esmé to keep her courage up. As the interview ended he said: 'Oh, Esmé, don't send in any pyjama trousers; I can't get them on over the chains.'

One month after this Esmé was herself arrested under the Ninety-Day law. On the day of her arrest Swanepoel went to Dennis to put his proposition once again. 'Tell us all you know,' he said, 'or we will arrest Esmé.'

The men arrested at Rivonia were taken out of their solitary cells on 9 October and brought to trial on charges of organizing sabotage and an armed uprising against the South African Government. Sisulu, Mbeki, Mhlaba, Kathrada, 'Rusty' Bernstein, Dennis Goldberg found to their surprise that Nelson Mandela was in the dock with them. Mandela had been serving a sentence of five years' for organizing the March 1961 strike and for leaving the country to speak for the African National Congress at the Addis Ababa P.A.F.M.E.C.S.A. conference, but despite this the Security Branch had put him under Ninety-Day detention as a preliminary to the strain of the trial. Also joined with them in the dock were cheerful rotund little Elias Motsoaeledi and tall silent Andrew Mlangeni, both just out of solitary detention cells.

*

Isolation in a Vacuum

I knew nothing of these events. I was shaken, though, when on Monday, 7 October, a smart navy-blue frock and matching coat with a red silk lining were sent in to Pretoria Prison with my laundered slacks and shirts, and soup in a thermos flask. This, I realized, was my mother's warning that I should expect to be taken to trial any day, and her equipment for me to mingle in the world again. But nothing happened. The next days went by in yawning emptiness.

From the time I was moved to Pretoria the visits by Nel, the Security Branch officer, had been perfunctory. On the average he came once a week; sometimes eight or nine days went by without a visit. Nel's air was one of bored indifference whether I talked to him or not. Sometimes his visits degenerated into brief sterile sessions of a formal inquiry and answer. 'Are you prepared to answer questions or make a statement?' 'No, I am not.'

Some days went by after the arrival of my blue dress and coat, and then one morning Nel had me brought down from the cell into the Matron's office and he opened the interview by saying, 'Well, Mrs Slovo, you have not been charged after all. Now you can talk.' I feigned ignorance. 'Charged with what?' I asked. 'Ah, come now,' he said, 'you know you were worried you would be charged in the Rivonia trial.'

This *had* been the worst of the worries. For the rest of the day and the night I breathed in great gasps of relief. I still did not know what was in store for me, but this was one hurdle taken.

I felt there was room now for me to manoeuvre in, and I began to agitate Nel to have me moved back to Johannesburg. I had no doubt that my shift to Pretoria had been to deepen my isolation, but it had also in part been anticipation that when I stood trial with the Rivonia men in a Pretoria court my cell would not be far away. Now courtroom and cell did not have to be near one another and the deathly stillness of Pretoria – I actually missed the hustle and tumult of Marshall Square Police Station – was eating away at my nerves. I told Nel how my ulcer was playing up and that erratic food deliveries from outside – my overtaxed mother had to travel thirty-six miles there and back to deliver a basket – were not making the situation any easier. I asked Nel to convey my request to Colonel Klindt. He said he would but I did not trust him to, so I asked for paper and pen, which he gave me, to my surprise, and I addressed a letter to the colonel asking for a 'transfer' back to Johannesburg.

Colonel Au'camp heard of this request and found it funny. Fancy a prisoner trying to arrange her own transfer; once you were in jail you stayed there until 'we' moved you, he said. He and I were having a wrangle of our own. I had asked to be allowed to purchase from the prison canteen, with my money locked in the Matron's safe, a tin of powdered milk called 'Klim' so that I could make a drink of coffee extract in my cell at night. He refused permission for the purchase. When I asked the reason he said 'Regulations'. The next time I saw him during an inspection I asked if I might read the regulations. He did not reply. One morning I was being interrogated by Nel in the Matron's office when the colonel walked in. I interrupted Nel to ask the colonel again for permission to buy the tin of 'Klim', and when he refused I asked him to give a reason. 'Security,' he said. 'Do you know what "Klim" is?' I asked. 'Yes,' he said, 'it's powdered milk, like babies use.' I appealed to Nel that babies' powdered milk could not endanger security, and there and then in front of me he told the colonel that he had no objection to my getting a tin. The colonel was unmoved. No 'Klim'.

Nel spoke a stilted awkward English. For the most part he stuck strictly to the purpose of his visit, digressing rarely. Once or twice he departed from the strict text. Bantustans would work, given time, he opined, and I disagreed vehemently and wanted to know if one of the purposes of my interrogation was to get me to accept the ideology of the Nationalist Party. I taxed him once with the arrest of my brother, Ronnie. This was after he had said that the Government used its Ninety-Day detention powers with unerring knowledge of who was a danger to the security of the State. 'My brother could not be called a danger to the security of the State,' I said angrily. The only chairmanship he had ever filled was that of a Johannesburg golf club. 'We don't arrest an innocent man,' was the reply. 'We know what we are doing. We assess every man before we make an arrest.' 'On the contrary,' I jeered. 'You arrest first, assess afterwards.'

(As it happened, my brother was released after three weeks in detention.)

Nel enjoyed his role as interrogator in his own cold, calculating way. He supervised the conditions of detention with quiet understanding and conscientiousness. When I protested about having nothing to read he said, 'If you have something to read you will not think about my questions, Mrs Slovo.'

When I grew angry and protested at my continuous imprisonment Nel taunted me with the Security Branch formula: 'We're not holding you, you're holding yourself. You have the key to your release. Answer our questions, tell us what we want to know, and you will turn the key in the door. Make a statement and in no time you will be back with your children.'

They would not permit me to see the children in Pretoria. One morning Nel arrived and opened the interview with, 'I see in the Sunday papers that your children are being taken overseas.' As he had hoped, I was immediately in a state of agitation. When, I asked, when were they leaving? He knew nothing except that the news of their impending departure had been carried in newspaper columns. 'I must see them before they go,' I said. 'Will you let me see them?' 'Why do you want to see them?' he asked. 'You have seen them already.' I took a deep breath. 'You,' I said, 'are a cold-blooded callous fish of a man.' 'Why do you say I'm a fish?' he muttered.

I had not been aware that solitude was giving me a craving for conversation, any conversation, even with a detective, and one day, to my consternation, I found that his question, 'What were you doing in South West Africa?' set me off on a round of inconsequential anecdotes and jokes. I chattered and he listened intently and suddenly took me up on my remark, 'But surely you know all this. ...? You know exactly where I went and what I did ... you had me followed all the time.' How did I know I was being followed, he wanted to know. I had seen the Security Branch men, I told him. 'Couldn't you have been mistaken? If you saw me in the street would you know I was Security Branch?' 'Yes,' I said emphatically and he looked disconcerted.

Nel and the Matron exchanged niceties one morning when she handed him a cup of tea through the open window during one of his visits. I was not listening to their conversation and heard nothing but the last sentence of the matron: '*Ag, nee, Meneer is nog 'n klein seuntjie.*' [Oh no, sir, you are still a youngster.]

He whipped round to me thinking I had overheard.

'You think I'm just a little boy, don't you, Mrs Slovo?'

'I don't think about you,' I lied.

'Would you prefer someone else to question you?'

'It makes no earthly difference to me,' I said, but I thought, Oh, for someone else. Anyone but this bloodless, impassive man.

Relations between us continued in a state of unexpressed enmity, except for my one outburst about his callousness. He wanted to know what secret meetings I had been to, who had been at them, who supplied the money spent by the Congress movement, who kept it, where it was kept, what went on in inner Congress circles, who 'gave the orders', what plans there were for the future. I had been a journalist, I said. Everything I knew about I had written up in our columns; he should consult the files. Make a statement, he urged me. Tell about the money. I knew nothing about any money, I told him. 'If they didn't tell you about the money they couldn't have trusted you?' Nel said. 'Trust me with money? No, I suppose not. I'm notoriously extravagant,' I said irrelevantly.

He told me once that he thought I had wasted my life. I might have done so much. I didn't agree, I told him, everything I had done I would willingly do again.

I was taken out of my cell one morning to meet not Nel, but my mother. The Grays had granted permission for an interview to discuss business and family affairs only. The detective sitting in on the interview was from Pretoria's Security Branch staff, he knew nothing of me, and was not very interested. I asked my mother if she was taking the children out of the country. She had made no such plans yet, she said, and she knew nothing of a report to that effect in any newspaper. She had news of a different kind. Colonel Klindt was away on leave but his deputy, Colonel Venter, had told her that I was to face a charge at the end of the ninety days. I could barely ask but I did. 'What charge?' Possession of illegal literature, it seemed, and once more I was enormously relieved. But if this was their intention, why hold me until the end of the ninety days? My mother said that she had put the same question to Colonel Venter but he had ignored her. We had a jolly interview, my mother telling me that my brother had been released, and that my father was safely out of the country.

I had seven days to go before the end of ninety days. That week I found I was talking to myself, repeating over and over again, 'Now, then, get a hold on yourself. These last days will drag worse than any other. Take it easy. Try to coast through the time, not long now . . . and whatever happens you've made the first ninety days. Don't build your hopes too high; be ready for a let-down. The chances are they will not let you go.'

Six days before the end of ninety days I was walking among the washing lines during exercise time when the Assistant-Matron unlocked the yard door, beckoned to me and said I should pack my things, I was being taken away. There was no sense in my asking questions; she did not know the answers and if she had known she would not have told me.

I packed my suitcase to the accompaniment of a thumping heart. In twenty minutes two wardresses took me down to the Matron's office. The colonel was there, and two men I had not seen before, one with a pimple-scarred face, the other with light-brown hair receding on an asymmetrical skull. I was breezy and cheerful. 'Where are we going?' I asked them. 'To Johannesburg,' they said. 'But where in Johannesburg?' I insisted. 'There are so many places in Johannesburg, among

85

them my home.' The fairer of the two men answered. 'I'm afraid you're not going to your home this trip,' he said.

The colonel teased me on the way out about the tin of 'Klim'. 'Oh, yes,' I said, 'I hoped you were going to bring me a set of the jail regulations. I suspect you don't have any.' '*I* am the regulations,' he said, and waved good-bye with his stick.

The detectives carried my suitcase and odds and ends, signed for the custody of me from the Pretoria Central Prison and led me to their car. There I noticed, lying on the front seat, a bulky charge-sheet made out '*The State v. The National High Command*'. They said nothing about serving a charge on me and I said nothing and kept my eyes averted from the document. If they were going to charge me they would enjoy making me endure the suspense of the thirty-six mile journey to Johannesburg. If they were not going to charge me, the threatening nearness of the official charge would build my suspense anyway. Van der Merwe, the detective with the pimply face, took the wheel, and J. J. Viktor (the Js stood for Johannes Jacobus) turned in his seat to watch me during the journey as we set off in the direction of Johannesburg.

Chapter Four

PUTTING ON THE PRESSURE

Van der Merwe did little talking during the journey. He took the route to Johannesburg which happened to pass within half a mile of my house, but this might have been coincidence. It seemed that the two detectives knew a good deal about me.

'How's Joe?' asked Viktor.

'Why do you call him Joe?' I asked testily.

'I know him well, hasn't he told you?' Viktor proceeded to recount the story of how Joe had defended prostitutes in a criminal prosecution and it had turned out midway through the magistrate's court trial that police evidence had been collected at the instigation and *with the money* of a rival school of prostitutes. Phyllis Peake, head of the most flourishing establishment in Johannesburg, had been determined to get upstart rivals out of business; well provided with police contacts, she had helped plan the operation in which policemen, in plain-clothes, or, more appropriately, with nothing on at all, had been surprised in bed with ladies of the rival establishment by other policemen – correctly dressed. Joe brought it out in open court and the town tittered at the salacious complicity of the police in helping Phyllis Peake sustain her profits. Phyllis Peake's ladies were livid. They had been in court and had been forced to listen as the unsavoury plot was revealed, but as soon as the court rose they gripped their stiletto-heel shoes in their hands, brandished their umbrellas and set off down the corridors of the magistrate's court to deal with Joe. He saw the troop advancing on him and stood hesitating. A door opened behind him, a detective leaned out and said: 'This way, Slovo,' and, knowing the lay-out of the court building, led him out of another exit.

I had not recalled who the saviour-detective had been. Viktor claimed the honour and seemed proud of the episode.

Van der Merwe lodged a claim too. He knew the lay-out of

87

our house, he said; he knew we had been on holiday in December 1957. He had been temporarily attached to the investigation staff of the Linden Police Station and had investigated a burglary of our week's washing which had been left in a small outside room at the back of the house.

Viktor said that neither he nor Van der Merwe belonged to the Security Branch. They were attached to Marshall Square and were temporarily on loan. He was normally part of the fraud squad; Van der Merwe was murder squad. They were looking forward to going home.

There was conversation during the drive back – unlike the drive to Pretoria when Nel and Van Rensburg had ignored me after the start of the journey and after a few of their barbed remarks had gone home. But between Viktor and me there was an atmosphere of bristling animosity. He was provocative; I was waspish. And felt all the better for it.

As we drove past the new South African Air Force monument, a jagged concrete wing stabbing the sky, he asked if I had ever considered how useful it could be.

'Useful for what?'

"You could get a good view from it for military intelligence.'

'Oh, how stupid can you get?' I snorted impatiently.

I delivered myself of a tirade against the sadistic use of solitary confinement and the denial of reading material.

'What would you read if we let you?' asked Viktor. 'Isn't the Bible good enough for you?'

Somehow we got on to brandy. Viktor wrote on the back of his cigarette-box the name of a brand I recommended. By now I realized I was going back to Marshall Square and the thought of a jail I knew was infinitely more comforting, however unpleasant those cells really were, than one I did not. When I was led to the counter of the charge office where I was booked in as a prisoner and I saw the face of the sergeant I had known from my last stay there, I forget myself and cried.

'Oh, home again!'

'Home?' queried Viktor, with a frown.

'Yes,' I said gaily. 'And if you come again bring a bottle of that brandy.'

The cell warder who took me to the women's section gave me the choice of cells, and from this I deduced that Hazel had been released and I was the only white woman in Ninety-Day detention. I could go back to my old cell on the edge of the Marshall Street pavement, or I could take the cell, cut off from the others, that was in the tiny women's exercise yard. 'Take that one,' the warder urged. 'It's the lucky cell; Mrs Goldreich was released from it.'

I decided that the warder had more confidence in luck than I, but I took his advice. I unpacked and settled in. The cell was somewhat larger than my former one, and it was less sooty and noisy. I didn't notice the passage of that day. I lay thinking about Hazel and the thrill of her release; though it had taken place about a month earlier, this was the first news I had of it. The Marshall Square routine came into play again, and as the cell door opened for shift changes and inspections I greeted familiar faces and was comforted.

Business at the station seemed slack that week and I was the only occupant not only of the cells used for solitary detention, but of the entire women's section. I could take my time over my wash the next morning, use both the bucket of hot water and the shower and, most exciting of all, I could creep into my former, now vacant cell, climb on the bedstead and crane my neck round the electric light pole to read the day's news poster.

As though in celebration of my return to Johannesburg the news vendor had planted the poster full face towards me. They were short words, centred, and there was no doubt what they said. But what could they mean?

DEAD

MAN

BANNED

*

Looksmart Solwandle Ngudle was his name. Looksmart because that was the impression he gave: resilient, resourceful, optimistic.

89

Ngudle was his family name. Solwandle was the name of the family that had part adopted and educated him. He had been one of the live-wires of the Cape Town African National Congress, the political organizer whom no hardship could subdue, his associates were convinced.

The Ninety-Day law was promulgated in May. On 19 August Looksmart was detained. On 5 September, sixteen days later, he was found dead in his cell. A short news item to this effect appeared in the daily Press.

Looksmart was the eldest son of sixty-year-old Mrs Maria Ngudle. She lived in Middledrift in the Transkei. On 15 September a policeman came to see her. 'You know,' he said, 'your son was arrested.' (She did not know. This was the first news she had of Looksmart's detention.) 'We are instructed to say that he has passed away in Pretoria.' Mrs Ngudle went for help to the African attorney in Middledrift. But he too had been detained under the Ninety-Day law. She went farther afield, to lawyers in Alice. Five days later, on 20 September, a rail warrant to Pretoria arrived for her. She left immediately and arrived in the capital on a Sunday morning.

'I was going alone looking for this place,' she said. 'I was shown the prison in Pretoria by some people. I said to the African policeman, "I have come for Looksmart's funeral." The policeman took down my name. He asked me if Looksmart was sentenced to death. I said I did not know, I only knew he was arrested. The policeman said he would go and look. He came back. " We have buried him already because we can't keep a dead person. How can we help you?" I said, "I want his clothes." He said there were none. He gave me a note to another prison. Again there I was asked if he was sentenced to death. I said I did not know. I was sent back to the other prison. I was seen by the same policeman who had seen me before. I was sent upstairs to some white policemen. I felt they were playing the fool. I went home. I could not find out what the cause of death was.'

Attorneys took over. In Johannesburg Joel Carlson sat on the telephone. The Prisons Department, the police, were evasive. No one seemed to know where Looksmart had been buried. Reference to a high authority was referred, in turn, to a yet higher one. Once, during a telephone conversation, a senior Prisons Department spokesman dropped his guard. 'Do me a favour,' he said, 'Go to the Security Branch.'

A date was finally fixed for an inquest. Suddenly it was postponed for eight days. More suddenly still it was brought forward ten days and the attorney was given forty-eight hours' notice that the matter was proceeding earlier 'on instructions of a higher authority'.

Advocate George Lowen had been briefed: 'The deceased in this case was a Ninety-Day detainee. A man in good health . . . who was found dead in a cell. News of his death aroused widespread unease because there is a curtain of silence hanging over those people detained. . . . The news was given to his family only ten days after his death. . . . The mother was given a rail warrant to attend the funeral of her son in Pretoria. . . . When she got there she was told the body had already been buried. . . . The burial had taken place on 16 September after the body had been kept for at least ten days . . . but then was buried suddenly in spite of the issue of the rail warrant to the mother. . . .' Why had the inquest been delayed, then rushed to court? There had been no time to gather witnesses or medical advisers, no time to take proper instructions. 'We don't know if this was murder or suicide. It is very strange that so much darkness is hanging over the whole affair.'

The plea for a postponement was granted.

In the intervening ten days two things happened.

Security Branch detectives arrived unannounced at Middledrift, put Beauty Ngudle, Looksmart's widow, into their car and drove towards Pretoria. Along the way they produced a statement for her to sign, that she had no wish to be legally represented.

On a Monday morning the court assembled at 10.30. The Prosecutor queried the locus standi *of the instructing attorney. In his hand he held the sheet of paper with Beauty Ngudle's signature on it. The attorney held a sheet of paper in his hand; it had been delivered to him in court only fifteen minutes earlier. It was an affidavit from Looksmart's brother, Washington, saying that he did want to be represented by the attorney. The Prosecutor conceded.*

Two days before the inquest was due to be resumed, Johannesburg's evening newspaper published the 'Dead Man Banned' news, that Looksmart Solwandle Ngudle had been banned under the Suppression of Communism Act. The Government Gazette announcement was dated 25 October, but the ban had actually been served on 19 August, the day that Ngudle had been detained.

Lutuli, Mandela, Sisulu, Slovo, Dadoo, Bunting, Alex La Guma, Lilian Ngoyi, Ronald Segal, Patrick Duncan, Helen Joseph, Dr Jack Simons, several hundred South Africans, Communist and non-Communist, even anti-Communist, had been banned under the Suppression of Communism Act. This meant that they could be arrested if they took part in any political activity or attended a gathering. It also meant that no statement by them, on any topic whatsoever, could be quoted or published. In the Ngudle inquest it meant, said counsel, that 'nothing which was ever stated by the deceased or by anybody else who was banned, can be quoted. . . . We have to withdraw from these proceedings with the utmost regret.' The only evidence of the circumstances which might have led to Ngudle's death would be the testimony of banned persons, fellow-prisoners of the dead man. How could such testimony be produced in court if there was fear that prosecutions would ensue?

The Minister of Justice, Mr Vorster, claimed that the withdrawal of the lawyers had been for political reasons. A court, as a privileged forum, could hear statements by the banned, and an inquest proceeding was a court. In the inquest proceedings themselves, there had been long argument over this. Then at last the Minister announced that he would permit the publication of statements by banned persons in inquest proceedings providing that the proceedings were not used as a political forum.

Suddenly the stillness enveloping the fate of the detained in their cells was broken. The bush telegraph in the jails began to work. It was November and detainees arrested between June and October in many parts of the country were being centralized in Pretoria prison; those scattered by twos and threes in different police stations were being taken to Police Central Barracks for interrogation. Interrogation under torture.

By some irrepressible process the start of the Ngudle inquest suddenly opened windows into rows of cells. The trickle of information was cautious, hesitant. J.T. was arrested in the same Elsies River house as Looksmart; they had been held in Cape Town cells at first, then been driven by car to Pretoria. 'Looksmart looked all right when I saw him but when he arrived at Laingsburg to get petrol, Looksmart told me his body was sore. He said that he had been beaten by the police that morning at Caledon Square Police Station.' In Pretoria T. had been separated from Looksmart, but on the following day they had met again to have their fingerprints taken and, 'Looksmart appeared to be in good health.' Five days later T. was taken into a room for questioning. 'I saw Looksmart leaning against the wall next to the door that I went through. We did not speak to one another. Looksmart did not seem himself. He looked paralysed. His head was bent forward and his hands were clasped together. I did not notice any bruises on his face. I did not notice whether his clothes were bloodstained. He looked worried. When I came out of the room after approximately one and a half hours Looksmart was no longer there. I never saw Looksmart again.'

Seven days after that Looksmart was seen by L.M. They had both been taken to the Central Police Barracks. 'I saw Looksmart with six Security Branchers, whites, and an African Security Brancher. They were standing next to me. I could see and hear it all. One Security Branch man was from Cape Town. The first thing I heard was: "If you talk you will be allowed to go." He, Looksmart, was looking down. He looked as if he did not know which one to answer. They were all asking him questions. The Cape Town one said, "You must tell us the truth or else tomorrow you will be here again and if you don't tell us the truth we will kill you." He was speaking in English. Looksmart did not answer. He never said a word. Then the Cape Town one pulled his beard and said, "You must tell the truth." They pulled his head up and down. Looksmart had been looking down. When his beard was pulled he moved back a bit but he said nothing.

Then the Cape Town one said, "Go and think it over and we will see you tomorrow." We were taken out together and I asked Looksmart in Xhosa what was wròng. He said, "These people say they will kill me tomorrow" . . . in the car I made a sign to him saying, "Did you make a statement?" He shook his head indicating "No." I gave Looksmart cigarettes without the Security Branch man seeing. He said, "Man, I don't know what's going to happen tomorrow." He seemed very worried about tomorrow.'

By the time that the inquest was resumed on 26 November, Advocate Vernon Berrange was representing Looksmart's relatives, and he had the statement of a prize witness up his sleeve. This was Isaac Tlale, the man who had been handcuffed to Looksmart during a torture session. The very first revelations of the torture of Ninety-Day detainees had been carried not in South Africa but in the British Observer of 3 November. The Commissioner of Prisons had dismissed the extracts of statements by prisoners as 'utter nonsense'. The statements, said General J. M. Keevy, Commissioner of Police, were 'a lot of bunkum'.

When the inquest proceedings opened Vernon Berrange set to work cross-examining the police witnesses brought to court by the State. They included Detective-Sergeant Ferreira, Detective Strumpher, Major Frederick Van Niekerk. It was established that detainees were generally taken for questioning to Pretoria Central Station; that there were about fourteen members of the Security Branch then working on the questioning of suspects. Strumpher said Looksmart had 'become a coward'. Not, he insisted under cross-examination, because of the treatment to which he was being subjected. The day before Looksmart's death Strumpher had handed the prisoner over to Detective-Sergeant Ferreira. It was Ferreira who had originally arrested Looksmart and had seized from his hide-out African National Congress booklets, a typewriter, rubber gloves, chemicals, and plastic bags.

Berrange cross-examined Ferreira in detail about the progress of the interrogation sessions with Looksmart.

'When he was told he would be charged with sabotage Looksmart admitted nothing?' – 'He was warned in terms of the judges' rules.'

'*Now, he had elected to say nothing and then it was decided to arrest him for ninety days?*' – '*That is so.*'

'*In the hope that you would be able to get him to say something about other people?*' – '*In an attempt to solve the sabotage cases in the Cape.*'

'*So he was detained in terms of ninety days in the hope that you would be able to get him to implicate other people in regard to acts of sabotage in the Cape?*' – '*That is so.*'

'*And indeed you had such strong evidence against this man you weren't in the slightest bit interested whether he made a confession about his own misdeeds or not?*' – '*No.*'

'*You wanted evidence about other people?*' – '*That is so.*'

'*And in order to get such evidence it was considered that it would be a good thing to lock him up for ninety days?*' – '*That is so.*'

'*You first suggested to him that he make a statement that would implicate other people on 4 September?*' – '*Yes.*'

'*He had already been taken from Pretoria North to the Central Police Station on six different occasions?*' – '*Five.*'

'*On 27 August what did you talk to him about?*' – '*About his health, his well-being, whether he wanted to write to his wife, etc.*'

'*Not one word passes your lips in which you say to him, " Now, Looksmart, are you prepared to implicate your friends?"*' – '*That's quite right.*'

'*You wanted to gain his confidence first by kindness?*' – '*That is so.*'

In the following days Looksmart was photographed and he was taken before two policemen who showed him certain exhibits and pressed him to say who had made them. One of the policemen had a list of names of people about whom he wanted information. Looksmart was still being stubborn, said Ferreira.

Berrange resumed:

'*And then suddenly on the 4th, the next visit, he told you – up to this stage you had got nothing out of him – then for the first time he suddenly said to you " I'm prepared to talk"?*' – '*That is right.*'

What brought on the change, Berrange demanded? Ferreira

denied that Looksmart had been ill-treated, that he had undergone torture, that electrical devices had been used to make him talk.

'He had suddenly become a coward?' – *'Yes.'*

'You don't know why?' – *'Why? I don't know why.'*

'You don't know why. It's a mystery to you. I think the time has now come for me to put to you the type of evidence that I'm going to produce to this court; and that evidence will be to the effect, and I want to tell you that I've got twenty witnesses who will testify to this, twenty, that during the time of their detention . . . when they were taken . . . to Pretoria Central, each and every one of them was subjected to the most gross brutalities. You know nothing about that?' – *'No.'*

Major Frederick Van Niekerk was the next policeman in the witness-box.

'This man Looksmart was obviously regarded by your department as being a person who could give a tremendous amount of information?' – *'He was regarded as the key figure, yes.'*

'Therefore the police would have regarded it as highly important for them to be able to get him to talk?' – *'It would have eased matters for us a great deal had he talked. . . .'*

'If a detainee, this man or any other, on being interrogated after he has been detained says, "I am not under any circumstances prepared to give you any information whatsoever", do you leave him alone or do you take further steps?' – *'Well, he has got to be asked again.'*

'And again?' – *'Yes.'*

'And again?' – *'Yes.'*

'And again?' – *'Yes.'*

'And again?' – *'Yes.'*

'I see, the idea is to wear him down, I suppose?' – *'I make no comment.'*

'What is the idea? You give me your comment.' – *'Well, he is there to give information, that's why he is detained.'*

'But if he has said to you, "Even if I've got it, I won't tell you"? Are these repeated interrogations for the purpose of wearing him down?' – *'No.'*

'*Well, what are they for?*' – '*To extract information from him.*'

'*The idea is to keep on questioning him to see whether he will change his mind?*' – '*Yes.*'

'*Supposing we had a case of a suspect who was detained because you, the police, genuinely believed that he could give certain information and if in fact your belief was wrong and this man couldn't give information, would you keep on questioning him over and over again?*' – '*The question is whether we genuinely believed that he could give information?*'

'*Yes, I'm putting it on that basis.*' – '*I would question him, yes.*'

'*You would, over and over again?*' – '*Yes.*'

'*That would be a dreadful thing to happen to a man, wouldn't it, if in fact you were wrong?*' – '*Yes.*'

Mr Berrange called his first witness. It was Isaac Tlule, fifty-year-old general dealer from Alexandra Township, father of five children, Ninety-Day detainee.

'*For how many hours of the day were you kept locked in your cell?*' – '*Since I arrived at this place I was never allowed out of the cell.*'

'*What happened when your cell was cleaned?*' – '*I used to be provided with a broom, I used to sweep the cell, and when they bring in my food they usually take the rubbish out.*'

'*Were you allowed any time for exercise, half an hour or an hour for exercise?*' – '*No.*'

'*And what sort of food did you get?*' – '*A piece of bread.*'

'*What else did you get besides bread?*' – '*I used to live on bread alone.*'

Tlale began the account of how one day towards the end of August he had been taken to Pretoria Central Police Station where he was handcuffed to a chair and assaulted by one whom he called '*Baas Kappie*'. He had fallen from the chair, the leg of the chair had broken, and with this Baas Kappie had hit him on the head.

The Prosecutor rose to argue that this evidence was not relevant. '*We are not here concerned with what happened to other people; we are only concerned with the deceased.*'

Berrange: '*You will be able to see at a later stage the relevance of this.*' He continued leading Tlale's evidence.

'*Now you say that you were hit on the head with a portion of a chair, that you were taken by the throat and that you were kicked?*' – '*Yes.*'

'*And during this time what were they trying to get you to do?*' – '*They wanted me to admit that I am the person who organizes the recruiting for the business.*'

'*Thereafter were you taken anywhere else in the building?*' – '*They took me to another place.*'

'*Is it a room?*' – '*It is an office.*'

'*And who was in the office?*' – '*I found a Bantu male sitting in that office.*'

'*At that time did you know his name?*' – '*No.*'

'*Did you learn his name later on?*' – '*Yes.*'

'*And what, later on, did you find his name to be?*' – '*Looksmart.*'

'*Now after you had been taken into this place which you call an office in which you found Looksmart sitting, were you then called to another room?*' – '*I was then called to another room.*'

'*And what happened in the other room?*' – '*I found three Europeans in that room.*'

'*Yes, and what happened to you?*' – '*They asked me if I was still denying. I said I don't know anything. I was then asked to hop.*'

'*Indicate what you mean.*' (*Witness then indicates.*)

'*I see, did you do that until you got tired?*' – '*I did that until I got tired.*'

'*And were you still denying?*' – '*I was still denying.*'

'*What were you then told to do?*' – '*I was told to undress.*'

'*Did you do so?*' – '*Yes, I did.*'

'*And then, where were you told to go?*' – '*I was handcuffed, there were two chairs which were joined together, I was asked to sit on those two chairs.*' (*Witness indicates.*) '*I was sitting in this way, my hands were handcuffed, in between my knees they inserted a broom handle, thick.*'

'*Below your knees and above your arms?*' – '*Above my arms and below my knees.*'

'So that you were pinioned then?' – 'Yes.'

'What happened to your head?' – 'My head was covered with a bag.'

'And what happened to your hands?' – 'I could feel that something was tied to my two small fingers.'

'And during this time you were being addressed, were they talking to you, asking you to do anything?' – 'They were asking me continuously whether I was still denying.'

'Did you continue to deny?' – 'I continued denying.'

'What was the next thing you felt?' – 'I then felt my body was burning. I felt as if something was shocking me.'

'Have you ever had an electric shock?' – 'Yes, I had it when I was repairing a motor-car.'

'The same sort of thing?' – 'Yes.'

'How many times can you remember were these shocks put through you?' – 'They did it twice.'

'What happened to you ultimately?' – 'Thereafter I lost my consciousness. The next thing I remember was standing next to a table signing a document.'

'Did anybody hold your hand?' – 'One constable was holding my hand.'

'Was this a document that had any writing on it or was it blank or what was it?' – 'I could see on this piece of paper on top was written my name and address.'

'And the rest, was it blank or had it writing on?' – 'It was blank.'

'And the sheet of paper on which you signed your name, was that the same sheet of paper, or can't you remember?' – 'It was not the paper which had my name on it.'

'And thereafter where did you go?' – 'They said I should go and clean myself.'

'Why did you have to go and clean yourself?' – 'I had messed myself up.'

'You defecated into your trousers?' – 'Yes ... I was taken to a latrine, I took a piece of paper and wiped out my trousers.'

'And then you were taken back to your room in which you found this man whom you later found to be Looksmart?' – 'Yes.'

'What happened to him?' – 'The constable called him by name

99

and said, "Looksmart come." It was then that I knew the name was Looksmart.'

'*Did he go to the room from which you had come?'* – '*When he left this room he went in the same direction that I had gone to.'*

'*Was he away for any time?'* – '*He was away for quite a time, approximately thirty minutes.'*

'*And when he came back, how did he look?'* – '*When he came back he was full of sweat in his face.'*

'*What was the colour of his face, had the colour undergone any change?'* – '*His colour had changed to green.'*

'*He looked green and did he look well or did he look sick?'* – '*He looked sick.'*

'*And where did he come and sit?'* – '*He came and sat in front of me, next to me.'*

'*Were you manacled, were you handcuffed, or were your hands free?'* – '*I was handcuffed, one hand was then made loose and they handcuffed one of Looksmart's hands.'*

'*The two of you were then handcuffed together?'* – '*We were then handcuffed together.'*

'*What did he say to you when he came to you?'* – '*He then asked me whether I came from the electric.'*

'*Yes, and what did you say?'* – '*I said yes.'*

'*And in that time had anything been brought to you to eat?'* – '*They brought fish and bread.'*

'*Did he eat any food?'* – '*He did not eat.'*

'*Did you ask him why?'* – '*I asked him why and he said this electric gave him some pain.'*

'*Would you give the exact words, because you gave them to me when I interviewed you. When you asked him why he didn't eat, what were the words he used? Please give the words in Xhosa.'* (*Words in Xhosa given.*)

'*What does that mean?'* – '*That means, "It's hurting me very bad."'*

Tlale said he was questioned on numbers of occasions and was told that if he did not 'admit' he would be kept in jail for ten, twenty, up to thirty years, and would be killed.

Putting on the Pressure

(Isaac Tlale was taken from court back to his cell. Some months later he was brought to trial with two other members of the African National Congress. The evidence against him, his defence lawyer said, was slight and contradictory. Tlale refused to go into the witness-box to clear himself, because he anticipated that the Prosecutor would ask him questions that might have implicated others, and he refused to be a party to that process. He was found guilty and sentenced to eleven years' hard labour. He is still in prison.)

The inquest proceedings adjourned and then re-convened to inspect the state of Zephaniah Mothopeng, teacher of mathematics, science and music, and close friend since their student days of the writer Ezekiel Mphahlele. Mothopeng had been arrested after Sharpeville and had served a two-year prison sentence. A year later he was arrested again, but his case was postponed in the cells below the Johannesburg magistrate's court without his being brought into open court. Four months later he was brought to trial, but the charge was withdrawn. Then, immediately afterwards, he was arrested again, and told that he was being detained for ninety days. He was pressed to give evidence against the Reverend Arthur Blaxall, who was charged with paying monies to the illegal Pan-Africanist Congress, but Mothopeng refused. He got the full torture treatment after that. He had been told that someone else had been killed in the room where he was being given electric shocks and that he too would be killed and his body thrown away, and no one would know about it. He felt he was 'going off my head'. He found himself in the jail hospital. The inquest proceedings were convened in the prison where Mothopeng was later confined, and the medical assessors recorded, 'Court inspects his fingers. Base of the index finger on the dorsal aspect is a superficial lesion of the nature of a superficial erosion approximately five mm. in diameter, etc., etc.'

Mr L. told the court that he had been taken to the mortuary to identify Looksmart's body. One of the police officers said to him, 'We are at war and your life really means nothing.'

By this time the inquest court had become restive. The evidence of the conditions and treatment of other detainees was irrelevant,

*the Prosecutor argued. The court ruled that evidence called by
Mr Berrange was inadmissible.*

*Berrange protested. 'I, at the inception of these proceedings,
made it clear that I proposed to call evidence to establish a brutal
system of ill-treatment by the police of prisoners in Ninety-Day
detention. In view of Your Worship's ruling it now becomes
apparent that not only am I prevented from leading this evidence
of a systematic technique of torture on other prisoners, but also
that the evidence of Mr Tlale now becomes inadmissible and
irrelevant. I have no option but to withdraw from these proceedings.'*

*The magistrate returned a verdict that Looksmart Solwandle
Ngudle had committed suicide by hanging himself, and his death
was not due to 'any act or omission involving or amounting to an
offence on the part of any person'. The verdict ended the attempt
to produce further evidence of the treatment of detainees but it
was too late for officialdom to try to stifle that. Looksmart by his
death and Tlale by his courage had lifted the lid for the first time
on the systematic resort to the torture of Ninety-Day detainees
by the Security Branch.*

*

The detective who had me taken out of my cell on the first
morning after my return to Marshall Square brought not a
torture instrument, but a piece of bait. I was still in a state of
euphoria at being out of the numbing stagnation of Pretoria,
though nagging away at my mind and my nerves was the
knowledge that I now had only five days to go before the end of
ninety days. As I walked towards the interview room I saw
Viktor standing at the door. 'Did you bring the bottle?' I asked
him. He handed me a bottle. Not brandy but a small bottle of
eau-de-Cologne that must have dropped out of my handbag on
to the back seat of the police car in which I had been driven
from Pretoria. He had come for more purpose than just to
hand the bottle back, it seemed. He appeared anxious to talk.
He talked about himself. He was a keen member of the fraud
staff in the C.I.D. His finest hour had been the conviction he

had secured against 'Babyface' Goodwin, an old hand at fraudulent deals who had somehow achieved the forgery of a liberation warrant that had got him out of The Fort where he was being held for trial on a series of offences. Goodwin did a Houdini act not only out of prison but out of South Africa and he had managed to get into the United States, where Viktor had been sent to bring him back once the extradition order had been arranged. By then Goodwin had moved to Canada. Viktor cooled his heels in the States, and so cool were they that he even took himself to watch a session of the United Nations, though the picketing against South African apartheid incensed him. He was thirty-four years old, already a lieutenant, and his good results in the previous promotion examination in the force boded well for his future career as a policeman. He was keen to get back to the fraud staff, he said, he was not really at home with the Security Branch.

He didn't think I was really at home in a police station. Why didn't I get myself out of this mess? I need only answer questions, and I would be free. How did he know I knew anything? I asked. 'You know. You know *plenty*. I know that you know,' he said.

I let fly at Ninety-Day detention. The Security Branch followed me, opened my letters, tapped my telephone, compiled a dossier on me. Then they had me arrested. They were my jailers. They were my prosecutors and my persecutors. And he tried to persuade me that if I talked to him the Security Branch would sit in calm judgement in my case, act not only as prosecutor but as jury and judge, and come to a free and unprejudiced decision on my future. I trusted no undertakings of any kind by the Security Branch, I said. I simply did not trust them. And as for information, I knew nothing of any interest to them.

'If you know nothing,' said Viktor, 'that's all there is to it. You can't have it both ways.'

He had an idea to put to me. I knew, he said, that when I was arrested the police had found a copy of *Fighting Talk* in my house, and I knew that this was a banned publication in terms of the Suppression of Communism Act. Well, the Attorney-General preferred charges, and the matter of a trial for possession of illegal literature was strictly the decision of the Attorney-General, but it was not impossible that Colonel Klindt could put in a word for me.

'What sort of a word?' I asked.

Well, he didn't like bargaining and he was striking no bargain and making no conditions, but if I were prepared to answer questions and give information it might happen that the prosecution would be dropped.

'You're only a junior officer,' I said. 'How can you make a proposition for the Branch?'

He said he could. That was not good enough for me, I told him. I would prefer it if he went back to his superior, Colonel Klindt, and brought his seal to this proposition. Viktor said he would do that, and he would return the following, Saturday, morning.

No one came to see me on the Saturday. I reflected on the *naïveté* of the detective's proposition. Sunday was always a dead day in the cells. The men on duty put their feet up when no one was looking and read the Sunday comics once they had done the minimum of bookwork required of them and had admitted the few errant characters who got themselves into a jail on a Sunday. There was still no one in the women's cells, and the wardress let me out into the small courtyard and left me in the sun for longer than the stipulated hour. I was worrying about the outcome of the first ninety days, yet trying not to. The wardress unlocked the heavy door into the yard and I prepared to go back into the cell. 'No,' she said. 'Someone to see you.'

A Sunday visitor. It was Lieutenant Viktor, squeezing in duty on a Sunday between Church and midday dinner. He apologized that he had not called on the Saturday; he had been busy. But he had talked over with Colonel Klindt the matter he had discussed with me, and he was authorized by the colonel to say that he, Colonel Klindt, approved of the proposition.

I had visions of myself in the dock tried with possession of

illegal literature and revealing the shabby deals peddled by the
Security Branch; I wanted to be exactly accurate, so I asked
Viktor once again to outline the proposition. He did so, using
almost the identical phrasing he had used before.

'You're acting highly irregularly, don't you think?' I asked.

'Not at all,' he said. The police do not lay charges so could
not strike any bargain with me by agreeing not to lay a charge
in return for information. But there was nothing to stop the
Commissioner of Police from writing a letter to the Attorney-
General and saying, more or less: 'In case you are thinking of
charging Mrs Slovo, it might interest you to know that she is
cooperating nicely with the police.'

'No,' I said, 'I am not interested in any deal.'

I let myself go again on the subject of the rule of law and
Ninety-Day detention and Viktor listened closely and said he
could fully understand my point of view seen strictly from my,
not his, end. I said I didn't trust the Security Branch; perhaps,
he said, I had my reasons. But he would advise me to consider
my position very carefully; after all, there was nothing to say
that I would serve only one period of ninety days; would I
relish another ninety days in detention, and another after that?
. . . And then there was the matter of being in possession of
illegal literature. Viktor left.

The next morning was Monday and to my astonishment I
was called out for a visit from the children and my mother. I
was taken aback, but as I sped along the corridor to the little
interview room I said to myself, 'This is a bad sign, not a
good one. If they're planning to release you at the end of ninety
days, which is tomorrow, they would not grant a visit from the
children today.' I had no time to consider what they were
planning. The three bright faces rushed at me as I entered and
we had a fevered session of hugging, with the three taking turns
to sit on my lap with their arms round my neck. I don't know
why I permitted myself to say out loud what we were all thinking but I said to the detective, Sergeant K——, who sat in on the
interview, 'Tomorrow my ninety days is up. Are you going to

prosecute me?' The sergeant's reply was circumspect: he had not had any papers relating to a charge placed on his desk, he said. Robyn's eyes had sparkled at the words, 'ninety days ... up ... tomorrow.' I would be out in time for her birthday after all. I could not spoil the visit by uttering the caution which I above all needed, though I did not seem to realize it at the time: it's unlikely they'll let me out, hold tight for another spell of detention. Sergeant K—'s attention was diverted by someone who asked him to enter the visit in the official book. My mother sidled up to me. 'B—'s talking,' she whispered. 'Something has gone terribly wrong.'

Chapter Five

'NO PLACE FOR YOU'

When the visit was over a few seconds later I was taken back to the women's section and was about to go into my cell when the wardress said that as I had not yet had my exercise time I might as well take it right then. I sat on the ground, my back against the wall, and tried to stop myself shaking. If B. was talking, that put an end to my prospects of release. He knew so much about me: what I had gone to Rivonia for, who I had met there, some of the meetings – one in particular – that I had attended there, the people I was in touch with in the underground, the work they and I did together. Why had he broken down? How had he broken down? He had always struck me as controlled and confidently self-contained, unimaginative even, but that was all to the good in detention situations. Could he be reached at all? How could I possibly find out if among his revelations to the Security Branch he had included me? My pulse was beating fast and I found it difficult to think in sequence. I felt as though I had been poised on a high diving-board above a stretch of water, timing my take-off, when someone had suddenly pushed me. And in the hurtle downwards the water below had dried up.

I was trying to control my panic at such unexpected betrayal when the wardress appeared to call me out again. Above all else I needed to be left alone to think and regain calm. That morning there was a plot against my privacy, connived at by the wardress who kept calling me away from my thoughts, and, unwittingly, by my own friends, on our side.

When I got to the waiting-room Nel was waiting to see me. He had not come for over a week, since Viktor's appearance.

'I've come to tell you to pack your things, Mrs Slovo, I'm releasing you!'

The seconds ticked by.

'I don't believe you,' I burst out. 'You're going to re-arrest me.'

'I mean what I say,' Nel said. 'I've come to release you this morning.'

'Don't bluff me,' I shouted. 'Don't tell me one thing and do another. Don't make a farce of this thing. Don't talk of release if you mean something else.'

'I've come to release you, Mrs Slovo,' he said insistently.

The wardress had been hovering in the background. 'Don't be like that, Mrs Slovo,' she butted in and took me by the elbow. 'Here is your chance to go home. Come, I'll help you pack.'

Doubtfully I followed her into the cell but then I was consumed with the excitement of pushing my possessions into the suitcase and getting the lid to close, gathering the basket of dishes and thermos flask, changing out of slacks into my navy frock and coat, giving the wardress the box of dried fruit that had recently been sent into me. Laden with suitcase, basket, and flask I staggered through the heavy door leading into the lock-up section, which opened smoothly at the twist of the key by the cell warder, and then into the charge office. The sergeant at the desk had been alerted; he had the book open and was already writing out the liberation warrant. He looked pleased; I had decided that the better warders on the Marshall Square staff didn't really like this Ninety-Day detention. They were used to locking people up, but according to the old rules of the game, and to some of these men forty-eight hours without a charge was long enough, never mind what kind of prisoner you were. The sergeant did not ask for any details; he didn't need many for filling in the form. He looked to see that the carbon was working, then stamped the top sheet and the one underneath, ripped out the copy, and handed it to me.

In my hand was a certificate of release.

Nel was still there. 'You might have told me twenty minutes earlier,' I reproved him. 'I could have gone home with my family, and now where do I find a car? I don't think I even have a tickey* to telephone.'

* A threepenny-piece.

I asked if I could use the charge office telephone and the sergeant said no, but there was a public telephone box outside on the pavement. I fumbled in my purse (which had been handed to me together with other possessions kept in a prisoner's property bag). A man standing next to Nel who must have been Security Branch but whom I did not remember having seen before, came up and peered over my shoulder. 'Look,' he said, pointing to the corner of the purse, 'There's a tickey.' He seemed as pleased as I was to find it.

I fished out the coin and made a beeline for the telephone box outside. I was only half-way there when two men, whom I did know as Security Branch detectives, walked up to me.

'Just a minute, Mrs Slovo,' the spokesman said.

'What do you want now?' I demanded, and my mind and hearing were alerted to hear ... 'a charge under the Suppression of Communism Act for possession of illegal literature ...', or something which would hint at that, but he said:

'... another period of ninety days.'

The second detective grinned hugely from ear to ear.

In the charge office I was sickly silent and tight-lipped. Not till later in the month did I confront Nel with, 'I thought you said you were releasing me?' to hear his Jesuitical prevarication. 'I did release you. *I* didn't re-arrest you.'

I left the suitcase, the basket, and the thermos flask standing in the middle of the charge office floor, and stood at the door leading into the cells, waiting for it to be opened. The two detectives who had done the re-arrest were right behind me. They did not leave me when we reached the women's cells, not even when I stood in the courtyard and waited for the wardress to take over. They motioned to her to open the cell door and said, 'Come inside, Mrs Slovo,' then themselves clanged the door closed, more loudly than I had ever heard it, and snapped the padlock into place.

*

James April was arrested during a night raid on his home, and he was taken from bed, where he was ill with influenza, to

Capetown's Caledon Square. '. . . . *I couldn't walk in this cell, but had to content myself with walking on the bed. I did strenuous exercise in the mornings and light training in the evenings. During my detention the marked feature was the number of occasions I was summoned for questioning – exactly two. When I refused to answer questions they threatened to send me to Pretoria and told me that the chaps arrested at Rivonia would hang. The confinement to that small cell was nerve-racking and it was only the unpermitted conversation we detainees had with one another that kept our spirits high. When I stopped reading the Bible I found my thoughts drifting aimlessly and uncontrollably, and my mind became so numb that I could not think deeply or for long on any one topic. Loneliness gripped me . . . I became unsure of my political convictions especially when B. and L. were taken away. After the first abortive cross-examination by the Security Branch I was a bit shaken when it dawned on me that I could be kept for further periods if I retained my spirit of uncooperativeness. I was haunted . . . I did not have one night's sound sleep. I was rudely awakened to the screams of a detainee who shouted that his house was on fire in the early hours of the morning. The man was shouting like a madman which he finally and tragically became. This man, William Tsotso by name, was kept in solitary confinement for months and now he finally cracked. When I first met him in the bathroom he appeared sane and pleasant. Later he kept screaming for two days on end, refusing to come out of his cell or to accept any food. The police did not call in any doctors for they said he was play-acting in order to get out. Subsequently since Tsotso's cell was near the main road they were afraid that the public might hear him and so they asked me to change cells with him. I refused, for I could see the sinister motive in their suggestion. However, they got another fellow to change. Meanwhile Tsotso's condition, both mental and physical, deteriorated rapidly and the only help the warders could offer at that stage was a few kind words, followed by impatient insults. The captain who inspected the detainees took up a cynical attitude to Tsotso's condition at first, but was forced subsequently to summon a doctor. Soon afterwards Tsotso was taken away, to Valken-*

berg* I believe. Anyway I personally saw Tsotso in an emaciated state, lying on his mattress growling, with his food uneaten next to it. When Tsotso was taken away he once more screamed like a madman.

'These tragic happenings were greeted with stony silence by the rest of us. . . . Our morale suffered . . .

'My thoughts were preoccupied with trivialities . . . I burst very easily into laughter, my mind seemed befuddled . . .'

John Marinus Ferus was one of the earliest Ninety-Day detainees, arrested in May. The Security Branch told him he was a saboteur, misled by the Communists and the Jews. 'When we have finished with you,' a detective said, 'you will be nothing but a bag of bones. Don't think I swear in vain, so help me God.' The detective told the head warder at the jail: 'He's a hopeless case.'

'I was called for an interrogation session. I had better start talking, they said, because they knew a lot about me already. All my friends, they said, were telling them what they wanted to know. I had better talk if I wanted to save my skin. One thing I have experienced after a hectic interrogation session: that night I will have the worst of nightmares, sometimes I even woke from my own screams. It needed all my concentration to keep my nerves steady. One thing I noticed during this interrogation period is that you get so fed up that you feel very much tempted to say "yes" to everything they say just to be done with them. But of course it was not as easy as that. . . . The visits of the Security Branch became less and less until the last thirty days when they came only once a week. In this time I discovered that the more I cried the more relieved I felt. . . . With the end of ninety days in sight I became excited. I kept telling myself that I will be released, but deep in my mind I knew that it would not be the case. A week before my detention period was to end the detectives came to see me again. Sergeant L. had a triumphant smile on his face. He told me they had specially come to give me a last chance, to prove that they knew everything and that I was stupid not to make a statement myself. I must admit I felt shocked and terrified because

* A lunatic asylum in the Cape.

*what they read to me was to a great extent factual. . . . I pulled
myself together. Unlike the time when I was eagerly looking forward to the end of my detention, when I was back in my cell I
started wishing that it was still a long way off. The week-end went
by far too quickly for my liking. The Tuesday came and the head
warder came and told me to get all my things together. I asked
him if I was going to be released; he said he did not know. I
received my property and got into the Security Branch car which
was waiting for me. They told me they were only taking me for a
little drive. . . . Arriving at Tulbagh Police Station we stopped,
and I was ordered to go in. Lieutenant S. came out to meet us.
After discussing something with the detectives who had brought
me back, he told me that they were releasing me and I was now
free to go. I protested like hell that they brought me first to Tulbagh and then released me. I asked them how I was to get home
forty miles; but that, they said, was my business, and they did not
care. . . . When I stepped out of the police station I noticed a few
cops standing in the street so I decided to go round the back. As
soon as I got into the street I started running. But I did not know
the place so they soon caught up with me, and brought me back to
the police station, and took me to a cell in the back yard. It was a
very small yard with walls about twenty feet all around it. . . . They
locked me in a cell and then left. Suddenly it was very quiet for I
was the only prisoner there; I flung myself on the mat and started
to cry bitterly. . . . The thought of another ninety days was too
much.'*

*

Left to face my second round of ninety days I was filled with
loathing and bitterness against the Security Branch detectives
who had stage-managed my humiliating phony release and then
re-arrest; but I was also overcome, for perhaps the first time
since my initial arrest, by a wave of self-pity. I had said barely a
word throughout the cruel pantomime, because I didn't want to
give the detectives the satisfaction of an outburst that would
reveal my feelings; my instinct told me to keep a tight hold on
my emotions and to let no sound of them escape me, but it was
more than I could manage. I sat on the edge of the bed, still in

my navy outfit, and shook with sobs. My 'release' had been some time in mid-morning; by late afternoon I was still sitting in the same position. The heaving of my shoulders had stopped, but a tight pincer-feeling was growing in my stomach.

That reminded me. I had made an arrangement with my mother, furtively, when the back of the Security Branch detective had been turned away from us during a visit, that if at any time I rejected a basket of food, it would be a sign that I had embarked on a hunger strike, and glucose tablets should be sent in to me. I could not endure another period of ninety days as though I were taking the experience calmly, within my stride, as my due desserts at the hands of the Security Branch; I had to draw attention to my plight, and even if I were carried out of the cell on a stretcher, some fussing by jailers and doctors would be preferable to an isolation that was treated as my normal existence. When the basket of food came round at nightfall I called the cell warder back and told him to return the food, I did not want it, or any the following evening either.

If only I could have stood outside myself; if only I had not believed that I would always have the strength to do whatever I wanted and that emotional shock was something separate from and subordinate to my reason. This was no time, at the end of ninety days spent in solitary, to embark upon a hunger strike, certainly not with my ulcer already recording, with a steady dilating pain in my inside, the state of my nervous anxiety. I did not offer myself alarmingly overt symptoms to recognize the effect solitary had had on me. I suffered no claustrophobia, no ringing in the ears, no voices coming from the walls, no nightmares, no double vision, no hallucinations. Disorientation was calmness itself, without my knowing the full extent of it. I was lonely, I was anxious, I longed for human company; I had not yet thought that these were short cuts to a loss of discrimination which could be the stepping-stone to far more alarming reactions.

I lay awake the whole night. I worried without stop about the news that B. was talking. This, I thought, introduced a critical change into my own position. I could not stand the suspense any longer; I felt an irresistible urge to act, to lose no more time, to make some move to force a counter-move from the Security Branch. I felt that I would crumble if I stayed still any longer. I had to make some exploratory move, some searchings. What success had they had in making detainees talk? What were the sources of their information? Where was the leak? Was it a planted informer? Again and again I went over in my mind the names of those who had been at the meetings in the outhouse at Rivonia. I knew of one man who had informed; every one of the people he had given away was now out of the country or under arrest ... and I was in this cell. They had known when they arrested me that I had been at Rivonia. This had been the second question they had put to me at the second interrogation session. I had had ninety-one days of floating in suspense, hanging in indeterminate doom. I would rather hear a verdict than face continued suspension. How could I get events round me to move? For ninety-one days I had been stubbornly impenitent, obdurate in making no attempt to draw them on in their questioning of me. I was still stubbornly uncontrite but now my impatience was stretched to the point of snap. I could no longer bear to sit and wait while events moved around me; I had to provoke them. I would begin to show some interest in questioning. To find out what they knew, I told myself. To offer them the smallest crumb of useless information as a catalyst. Perhaps I would wait a week before the routine visit and question, 'Are you prepared to answer questions?' and I would then make a tentative move. I didn't have to. Nel arrived the following morning. I felt withered inside.

'You see, Mrs Slovo,' he said, 'we are persistent.'

There was silence for a while and then he asked if I would go to The Grays to answer questions. I said I would.

I remember nothing about the drive through the city in the back of a Volkswagen. I was taken to a room at the end of the corridor on the seventh floor. Viktor was standing apart from the others. He looked at me and said: 'Don't lose your nerve. Come on now, hold on.'

I hardly heard. I was packing my mind. Into a strong-room

section labelled 'NEVER to be divulged' I stored everything I knew – and I knew so much that I was heavy with it – which would provide trails to information the Security Branch so wanted. I was left with precious little: names of people either safely out of the country or beyond saving because they had already been caught and imprisoned and informed upon; information that we had partly divulged ourselves, in our Press, or which the mass organizations had made public knowledge. The police knew quite a lot about me; I might placate them with some more information that could not take them any further, seeing that B. and others had already talked.

There was activity in the room around me and when I looked up I saw Swanepoel arranging chairs and rigging up a tape recorder. 'Oh, no,' I said. 'Not a tape recorder.' A tape recorder would be quicker and more accurate, Swanepoel insisted. I could not speak on a tape, I said, it would make me nervous. I flatly refused. Viktor intervened. 'If she doesn't want a tape recorder, we'll do without it,' he said. He would take notes. He prepared a pile of foolscap and filled several fountain-pens from a bottle of ink that he took from a drawer. Van Zyl came into the room (Nel, Viktor and Swanepoel were already there) and Van der Merwe. I realized with a shock that this would be an interrogation session of a different calibre. I would not have just Nel or Viktor or even two of them together to fence with in evasion and half-statement; this was to be a fully-fledged examination. I got a further shock. There would be no questions. I was expected to make a statement, starting at the beginning, they said, and ending at the end, omitting nothing. I was asked to sit on a chair mid-way between Viktor, who sat with pen poised over paper, and Swanepoel who produced a thick file with my name on the outside 'Heloise Ruth Slovo née First' and began to go slowly and methodically through the great piles of paper in it, making notes as he went along on a stack of paper beside his right hand. Van der Merwe sat next to him, glancing from the notes that Swanepoel was making to my face. Van Zyl and Nel lurked in the background behind my chair.

I made a slow, comforting start. And what I told them about my awakening interest and steady involvement in politics seemed to be normal behaviour, the only thing to do in South Africa! We whites who embarked on protest politics side by side with the Africans, Indians, and Coloureds, led a vigorously provocative life. Our consciences were healthy in a society riddled with guilts. Yet as the years went by our small band led a more and more schizophrenic existence. There was the good living that white privilege brought, but simultaneously complete absorption in revolutionary politics and defiance of all the values of our own racial group. As the struggle grew sharper the privileges of membership in the white group were overwhelmed by the penalties of political participation.

I was born in Kensington, Johannesburg, and went up the road to Jeppe Girls' High School. My university years were cluttered with student societies, debates, mock trials, general meetings, and the hundred and one issues of war-time and postwar Johannesburg that returning ex-service students made so alive. On a South African campus, the student issues that matter are national issues.

Who had influenced me? they wanted to know. No one in particular. I had been able to read for myself. I didn't have any one teacher of politics; we students learnt from one another, and from what was happening around us. Manchuria, Abyssinia, Spain, Austria, Sudetenland, were not events of my own student generation, but they were close enough to influence us. There were Africans going to war carrying assegais and stretchers; there was bitterness that war-time costs of living were obliterating the buying-power of wages, that African trade unions were not recognized, that African strikes were illegal and the strikers prosecuted in mass trials.

I had graduated with a Social Science degree, but I turned my back firmly on the social worker's round of poor white families in Fordsburg, questioning them about what they did with their money to justify an application for State-aided butter or margarine. I landed up working for the Social Welfare Department of the Johannesburg City Council, Research Division, but expectations of research were dashed and I spent my days writing and editing the section headed 'Social Welfare' in a commemorative album for the city's fiftieth jubilee (this was 1946): checking the figures for the number of play supervisors for (white) children in (white) parks; the number of beggars still on the streets despite vigorous public relations work by the department to stop the public giving them alms; the number of work centres for the disabled and the handicapped (all white). The ambitions of the Director of Social Welfare had flown high: there came a time when he was invited to make a broadcast about the plans of the department, and I had to produce a sycophantic account of work which bored or disgusted me. When the African miners' strike of 1946 broke out and was dealt with by the Smuts Government as though it were red insurrection and not a claim by poverty-stricken migrant workers for a minimum wage of ten shillings a day, I asked for an interview with the Director and told him that I wanted to leave the department – without serving the customary notice laid down by municipal terms of employment. That was impossible, he said. Then he asked, 'Have you another job? What will you do if you leave here?' 'A political job,' I said. By the following morning I had permission, indeed the silent entreaty of the nervous Director, to leave the service of the department – without the required period of notice.

The time of the mine strike had been a tumultuous one. The strikers were enclosed in compounds under rule by the army, the mine, and state police. J. B. Marks, the union president, and all the officials and organizers of the African Mine Workers' Union, were being hunted by the police. A great squad of volunteers of all colours helped them set up strike headquarters in the most unlikely places, and from lodging rooms like the one I shared with a girl-friend, the handles of duplicating machines were turned through the night, while in the early hours before dawn white volunteers drove cars to the vicinity of the mine compounds and African organizers, hiding their city suits and their bundles of strike leaflets under colourful tribal blankets, wormed their way into the compounds. They and the army of migrant workers drawn from almost every country in the southern half of Africa kept the strike going for a climacteric week in South African labour and political history. The mine strike inaugurated a new period of militancy and a great surge forward of African political organization. The days of petitions and pleadings were well and truly over; the Government's puppet Native Representative Council adjourned in protest over the breaking of the strike, and never convened again.

When the mine strike was over I became a journalist. Our series of newspapers – for one was banned after the other, and there were times when we were hard pressed for new names to put on new mastheads – threw those of us working for them into the issues that rotted the lives of the African people: unceasing police raids and arrests, continuous removal schemes to try and sort white from black according to the precepts of segregation, forced labour on the farms, a daily multitude of persecutions and indignities. Sometimes our columns reflected what was happening; sometimes we initiated exposures that prompted new campaigns and gave our staff a reputation and a keenness for being first on the spot to write the news that no one else had the courage or will to print.

Up to six months before my detention I had still been in our newspaper office. Over the years I had been served with banning orders that prohibited me from leaving Johannesburg, so that I could take part in no further exposés of forced labour like my work on Bethal; from entering African townships, so that I could no longer personally establish the contacts of African men and women who alerted our office first of all when some new vicious scheme of the police and the administration came to light; from attending meetings, so that others had to take the notes and the photographs; from writing anything for publication, so that I had to sit at my desk with a legal opinion that sub-editing someone else's copy might just slip past the ban. Working in the midst of these ministerial bans and under the continuous raids and scrutiny of the Security Branch was like going to work each day in a mine field, but we survived, and our editions continued to come out each week. Then finally the bans stopped every literate or available Congressman from writing, and the printer, the last one we could find in the country to publish our notoriously outspoken copy, gave us notice that he could no longer take the risk. We sold the paper to a new proprietor whom we hoped would assemble a fresh team of writers. We were not to know until almost a year later but 'Babla' Saloojee, the new owner, was himself detained under the Ninety-Day law, and, driven to despair by the interrogation methods of the Security Branch, he hurled himself to his death from the window of the very room where I was being questioned

I told the detectives sitting like birds of prey over me the bare outlines of this story, stringing it out for as long as they showed patience to listen, for I did not know what I would say when we came to the end of all legal political activity for the African people and their allies in South Africa. The detectives were clearly not interested in most of what I told them, though Viktor took it all down without comment and at one point ordered a detective to leave the room and check somewhere in the records department of The Grays the dates on which the various papers had been banned.

The staff of our papers had reported the series of political strikes from 1950 onwards, the Defiance Campaign of 1952, the series of local resistance efforts by the people in towns and countryside, the treason trial – both Joe and I had sat in the dock – which began with Government bluster and ended in Government ignominy, the final peaceful attempt through the Mandela-led strike of 1961 to assert African claims for rights and self-government. The strike had been run without pickets, but it had been crushed by Saracen armoured cars fresh from duty a year before at Sharpeville, where the grotesquely sprawled bodies in the bright sunlight had shown the world the meaning of Nationalist rule, demonstrating to South Africans that you could not fight terror with spontaneous anger and appeals for a change of heart by the oppressor. On Dingaan's Day, 16 December 1962, when Afrikaners took part in folk-dancing to celebrate the defeat of Zulu military power at the Battle of Blood

River in Natal, a new organization, *Umkonto We Sizwe* [The Spear of the Nation] announced its formation from posters stuck on city lamp-posts, and a bomb went off in the hand of Molefe, the first sabotage casualty, to kill him as the new offensive opened. There were no longer public meetings at which Security Branch men could photograph speakers and audience; the police had to try to get their information by tapping telephones, trailing people to meetings, planting informers. They had little success . . . until Vorster promulgated the No Trial law with provision for detention, for ninety days or eternity, of anyone suspected by the police of having information.

In the legal period I had been active on our newspapers and in the Congress of Democrats, founded when the African National Congress needed an organization of whites who would support its policies and break the front of solid white reaction ranged against it. I had been abroad to the founding conferences of the World Federation of Democratic Youth and the International Union of Students; I had visited the Soviet Union and China (and Britain, Italy, Yugoslavia, Germany and France) and had written and edited booklets about them.

Why had I fled to Swaziland during the 1960 State of Emergency after Sharpeville? one of the detectives demanded to know. 'Because you would have arrested me without preferring a charge or bringing me to trial, like you did to 1,800 others,' I said. The Security Branch knew very well that I had spent emergency months in Swaziland; they did not know that I had come back to live underground in Johannesburg during the second half of the emergency, and I did not tell them.

I had been going to meetings throughout the period I was banned from taking part in political activities, I volunteered. I could even tell them what I had been doing at Rivonia. I had been to one meeting, an enlarged meeting of Congress activists to discuss and synchronize the range of political activities conducted by various divisions of the Congress movement. I had been to Rivonia for the very reason that motivated the activities of the Security Branch. Viktor looked interested at this point only. I was engaged in the collection of information. For writing purposes. I needed to interview the veteran Congressmen with whom I was banned from communicating in normal circumstances, and I had made regular attempts to meet them at the underground headquarters and interview them about their lives of political struggle.

Swanepoel went on making notes all the while. Viktor wrote evenly across the sheets of foolscap paper. The others listened. Towards the end they began to dart questions.

Who wrote articles in *Fighting Talk* under the pseudonym XXX, they wanted to know. I did, I said. (Though I had not.)

What about the Turok conviction for sabotage, after he had planted a bomb in the post office? 'I couldn't tell you,' I said. All I know about that was what I read in the newspapers. You might have asked my husband, he was one of the defence counsel, but now it's too late, isn't it, he's no longer here.'

'What did your husband do when he went out every night?' I couldn't say, I made a point of not asking him about his movements.'

'What about sabotage?' I was not involved in sabotage and I could tell them nothing about it, nothing at all; this had been something in which I had not got involved.

Who had I met most frequently at meetings? A. and E. and L., I said. (All out of reach of the Security Branch.)

Where had I been to meetings? In my house, in my motor-car parked in some quiet place, in the home of D. (long settled abroad).

'It's a funny thing, isn't it?' said Viktor. 'But every name you've given us is the name of someone who has left the country!'

'Perhaps they had good reason to go,' I murmured.

'What was discussed at that Rivonia meeting you attended?' The state of the Press, my chief interest, I said. The political situation in general. The trade-union movement. I was vague and bored as though every political meeting was the same and went laboriously over the same standard items on the agenda.

My statement had stopped with, to them, alarming unexpectedness. I don't know why my reactions were so appallingly slow but though I had decided at the outset that I would play out a small measure of the rope, it took the slow progress of the interview for me to realize fully that I was winding it fast around me. There was no time to wriggle, to fabricate, to gauge reaction, to probe, to find out anything for myself. I was breaking down my own resistance. It was madness for me to think I could protect myself in a session like this, in any session with them. I had no idea what they knew, what contradictory information they had wrenched from someone else. They were giving nothing away; they had already become too experienced for that.

It was now mid-afternoon. Viktor said that was enough for the day; he left the room.

Swanepoel sorted his notes, pinned them together, and tilted back his chair.

'You don't think that's a statement, do you?' he roared. 'You've told us nothing, absolutely nothing. You've not begun to talk. Those sheets are absolutely worthless. We know all about that meeting at Rivonia. It was a meeting of picked people from all over the country. Mandela was there, and Sisulu. The pick of the bunch. You're the only woman there . . and you try to pretend that you know nothing of what happened, that you can't remember, that nothing happened worth knowing. We know all about you. You'd be surprised to know what we know. You're deep in it. You can count your lucky stars that we still have respect for women in our country. You could have been charged in the Rivonia case. But we didn't want a woman in that case. We still have some feeling for women. We picked our accused. . . . We picked our witnesses . . .'

Swanepoel's face grew purple as he raged. The other detectives were now standing and watching me.

'You were in on that Rivonia thing from the very beginning,' he continued. 'What's more, we have a sworn statement that you paid Jelliman.'

'I paid Jelliman?' I echoed in disbelief.

'Yes, you paid Jelliman. It's in a sworn affidavit.'

Jelliman was an old man who had acted as a caretaker on the Rivonia property when Mandela had lived there in hiding at the start of his 'Black Pimpernel' existence. I knew Jelliman from the old days of legality; we had seen one another at Rivonia; I had never given him any money.

'What about Schermbrucker?' 'We've worked side by side in the same office for years. What else?'

'What about Beyleveld? There was an account from him in your cheque book?' 'His wife runs a typing agency, I've often had work done there.'

'What about Fischer?' 'Bram is a friend, a very dear friend of mine, a wonderful man, and – Thank God for the reputation of your people that you have at least one saving grace – he's an Afrikaner.'

Swanepoel went on the rampage again. 'I know you Communists by now,' he stormed. 'I've dealt with dozens of your kind. And I've learnt that they have to be put against a wall and squeezed, pushed and squeezed, into a corner. Then they change, and talk.'

The bombardment from Swanepoel split my bamboozlement wide open and it dropped from my head like a broken husk.

Perhaps Swanepoel's stable-mate, aspirin-and-ooze peddling Van Zyl saw it. He cut Swanepoel short as the latter was rising to a new peak of his harangue. It was late, he said, and I must be tired. I should be taken back to Marshall Square and they would resume in the morning.

Only now, when I was to be taken back to Marshall Square, did Viktor reappear. That was the end of any statement from me, I told him and the others still in the room. They said I had paid Jelliman, that there was even a sworn statement to that effect. That showed the quality of the evidence they had gathered against me. People under pressure of continued detention and threats would say anything to buy an indemnity, and I was in no doubt that the files of statements made by their victims were full of false information. I had again to protect myself from their persecution in the only way I knew: by remaining silent. 'Tomorrow,' they said. 'Tomorrow.'

I was taken back to Marshall Square. I was drained, prostrate with tiredness. But I could not sleep. I knew so clearly that I should make no statement, I could not understand – and I was too desolate to try – how I had allowed myself to think otherwise, even in a wild gamble for information and relief from solitariness. That was all I thought the entire night: literally two words 'NO STATEMENT NO STATEMENT NO STATEMENT' over and over again in my mind. I realized I had to eat again; perhaps my precipitate hunger-strike had helped to unhinge my judgement.

The next morning Viktor had me brought out again. As I walked towards him in the corridor I said, 'I'm not going back to The Grays. I am not making any statement.' 'You're not coming to The Grays?' he said. 'Pity. Your mother is there, waiting to see you. Colonel Klindt granted her request for a visit.'

I could not refuse to see her. Van der Merwe was with Viktor, driving the car, and on the way through the city he said, 'Why no 1—' and stopped himself. I knew what he was asking. Why had I put on no lipstick, no make-up that morning? This was the first time even in my detention, apart from the first day when I had no make-up because my suitcase was locked away, that I had permitted anyone to see me without make-up. I had simply forgotten that morning.

Viktor sat in on the visit with my mother, the first time an interrogator had extended his scrutiny to the effect of my visitors on me, and how we reacted to one another. My mother was upset; though to me it seemed a lifetime ago, it was only two days since I had been re-detained for a second spell, but her control was as superb as ever. We talked about the children, about the state of my father's health and how he was now safely in England, about her house which she was putting up for sale since it seemed she would continue to live in mine for some time to come. Viktor called the interview to a close after about twenty minutes, but allowed us to embrace. 'Are you cracking up?' she whispered, and I nodded. 'We're depending on you,' she said, and then she had to go. Viktor asked afterwards what she had whispered, and I said, '. . . something like "Keep your courage up."'

Viktor sat at his desk after the visit and got out the statement of the day before, as though to continue writing at my dictation. I told him I was not making any statement. 'This one is not finished, just finish it,' he invited. I refused. I gave some confused explanation: I was caught in a web of statements about me that they had taken from other people, statements which were not true. Jelliman's was an example of that. I did not trust the Security Branch and would not place myself in their hands; they were out to trap me.

'But we're not interested in you,' he insisted. 'We can't use what you tell us about yourself. We simply want to know what you know, and you will be perfectly safe.'

We went on and on in this vein. I was again limp with exhaustion.

Just before Viktor gave up and took me back to Marshall Square he leaned across the desk and said: 'There is a special reason why I want you to finish your statement and get out of here. I can't tell you what the reason is, but perhaps I will be able to one day.'

The following morning Viktor came again to fetch me to The Grays. I refused to go. 'Your sister-in-law is waiting to see you,' he said.

This was the first time that Clarice had managed a visit; again I agreed to go with him. Nel sat in on this interview and seemed surprised when I said: 'Oh Clarice, they'll never let me go, you watch . . . they just won't let me go.'

When Clarice had gone Viktor said that he had arranged for me to see Colonel Klindt; since he himself could not persuade me that the Branch was not interested in me, but only in what I could tell them about others, the colonel wanted to talk to me. The colonel was having coffee and he had a cup brought in for me; he fetched a tin of biscuits from a cupboard opposite his desk, and urged me to eat one, they were home-made, by his wife. He was prepared, he said, to give his absolute assurance that they were not interested in a conviction against me; I would be free to go. If I finished the statement he would personally engineer the fastest release so far from Ninety-Day detention; if by some chance I were not liberated immediately, he would go personally to the Minister to demand to know why not; he would stake his job and his official position on my case. I repeated that the only way I knew to protect myself in detention was by my silence. Klindt repeated his assurances, and said I should think the matter over again. He told me that Swanepoel's behaviour the afternoon of the first day I had been at The Grays had been reported to him, and he had 'taken steps'. He would brook no shouting or bullying by his men, he assured me.

Colonel Klindt made a gesture of good faith. On top of his desk lay a Penguin crossword puzzle book with my name written on it in my mother's handwriting: he must have had it in The Grays for months. He picked it up, paged through it and handed it to me. 'We're not all that inhuman after all,' he commented. An afterthought struck him. 'Have you a pencil?' he asked. I had no pencil. He had two fetched from next door, both indelible pencils with the words 'PROPERTY OF THE SOUTH AFRICAN ADMINISTRATION' printed on them, and he instructed Viktor to see that they were sharpened for me.

When we left the colonel's office Viktor, who had been at ramrod soldier attention throughout, said that he had never known the colonel or anyone in so senior a position stake his job on a prisoner as Klindt had done for me.

He took me back to his office where there were no detectives to be seen. I told him he was wasting his time and his patience, I was making no further statement. 'Will you sign this one?' he asked. I refused to do that. 'Would you like to tear it up?' he asked and when I said 'Yes,' he laughed and put it away in a drawer. 'I could tell you wanted to tear it up by the way you looked at it,' he said. I could not possibly incriminate myself, he stressed. Was I still worried about that? I said I was. 'If we release you, take you home, will you make a statement after that?' he sprang at me. I paused for a while. 'No,' I said. 'You will release me, but you can always take me in again.'

Viktor said : 'You don't really mean that. You're just staunch, you don't want to talk.'

Van der Merwe came into the office and the two of them drove me back to the police station. They asked me if I didn't want to see the sights of Johannesburg, and they took a round-about way through the city, past the new station building, the largest central park and the university area. Johannesburg had been changing since I 'went in' they explained. Investors abroad were showing confidence in the Nationalist Party Government even if I was not; a great multi-million pound hotel was going up on an old brewery site. They hoped I was enjoying the drive? I was not. I was deep in thought until suddenly it struck me that someone might see me riding about in a car with Security Branch detectives and draw the worst possible inference : that I had sold out and was now on their side. I asked to be taken back to the police station cell. They agreed, but suggested *en route* that they might one evening come to take me out for a film show at one of the drive-in cinemas.

I was appalled at the events of the last three days. They had beaten me. I had allowed myself to be beaten. I had pulled back from the brink just in time, but had it been in time? I was wide open to emotional blackmail, and the blackmailer was myself. They had tried for three months to find cracks in my armour and had found some. The search was still on. Some, many perhaps, of my weaknesses had been revealed to the Security Branch; if they had any inkling of others, I would have no reserves left. I could no longer hold to an intransigent stand because I had already moved from it. It was too late to say stoically that I would say nothing, not one word, to them. Nor did I want to say outright, 'To hell with the lot of you; the idea of telling you anything has driven me practically out of my mind.' I had too little emotional resilience left to resist a savage new onslaught on my vulnerable centre : that above all I was fighting to salvage my respect in myself, in the hope that my associates in the political movement could still preserve confidence in me. Viktor suspected this; but perhaps he was not absolutely sure that this was the point at which to attack me. If he had any hint of what was in my mind, I knew the Security Branch would spread reports that I had made a statement telling 'all', that I was broken and useless, had given in under pressure. I was in a state of collapse not for fear of what would happen to me physically, of numberless pealing days in detention, but for the gnawing ugly fear that they could destroy me among the people whose understanding and succour I most needed, and that once they had done that I would have nothing left to live for. I had not signed that useless statement, but it was nestling in Viktor's drawer, had probably been cyclostyled by now and placed in other dossiers, and might be brandished in front of some other detainees remaining silent. 'What's the good of holding out? Here's another one who has cracked and told us all.'

So I tried to give no hint of the trepidation I was in, and I ignored Viktor's finding that I was staunch to my ideals. I pretended a confused grasp of situations and the law; I kept repeating the same sentence with an illogical disregard for the context of the discussion. I could not talk any more because I would be giving myself away, I insisted, and somehow or other, I didn't know how, they would find a way to use my own statement against me. I decided to play the fluffy-minded frightened girl in a spot, given to inconsequential comment, with an inflexible inability to concentrate and grasp the essence of a problem.

My signs of cooperation had been utterly unconvincing; would the Security Branch be taken in by this subterfuge? Viktor had said: 'I was looking forward to meeting you. They said you were so tough'; but he and Van der Merwe had said about me, in front of me, the day they were bringing me back from my final session at The Grays, 'She's a nice girl.'

The trouble was that I did not take myself in by this subterfuge. Sleep had been a refuge in the cell; now it had fled. On top of sleeplessness I had nausea and diarrhoea. It all spelled anxiety, I suppose, but an anxiety that had got out of hand and that I could no longer control with my own resources. I asked for a visit from my own doctor. They sent a prison doctor first, one of those bumbling, beaten-by-police-regulations men who fitted fleeting visits to police station cells in between testing drunks for balance along a straight white line on the floor, and plunging a syringe into queues of holiday-makers bound for areas of possible smallpox, cholera, and yellow fever. This was one of the better prison doctors; he agreed with me that I should have a visit from my own doctor, and he signed some form, or gave permission, to that effect. My doctor came and was marvellously calm and normal, but I feared to embarrass him politically by too close an account of why I was in such an overwrought state. He gave me a mixture to control ulcer pangs and a phial of sleeping-pills.

I had the crossword puzzle book and I should have given in to gluttony and whipped through the puzzles, but I rationed myself to one puzzle a day. I had been given the book as an inducement to finish the statement, but I had no intention of doing that, and sooner or later they would take the book back as reprisal action; that at least. I had to make it last as long as possible, though, for I accepted that I now had no option but to adjust to indefinite detention, detention for eternity. I had never been afflicted by a fatalism quite so deep.

The days were grey and melancholy. I barely noticed the exercise periods. I had reeled back from a precipice of collapse but I felt worse than ever. I was persecuted by the dishonour of having made a statement, even the start of a statement. Give nothing, I had always believed; the more you give the more they think you know, and the more demanding they become. I had never planned to give anything, but how could I be the judge? It would be impossible to explain such an act, to live it down. Joe had always told me that my weakness was my extreme susceptibility to acceptance and fear of rejection and criticism: were these the qualities that had propelled me to make a statement? Or was it again my arrogance, my conceit that pooled experiences and rules of conduct (under interrogation) were for other people, and that I was different and could try my own way? My air of confidence had always been useful in keeping

129

others from knowing how easily assailed and self-consciously vulnerable I was; it had worked many a time, but it could do nothing for me now. I had presided over my collapse with a combination of knowingness and utter miscalculation. My conceit and self-centredness had at last undone me. I had thought to pit myself against the Security Branch in their own lair. What had I hoped to learn? To see dossiers carelessly littering desks, to hear the name-dropping of informants, to be taunted into giving information by the revelation, to surprise me, of what information they already had? I had been stupid. Weak. A failure. By day and by night I went over this self-exposure. I was a spider caught in my own web, spinning finer and finer threads in my head to make disentanglement impossible. I felt unimaginably tired and dispirited. I could not cope any longer. I could not weigh up factors properly. No one could get near me to help me and the help I needed could not be supplied by anyone else. I spent all Sunday making a dilatory attempt at a crossword puzzle, but filling in the clues was surface activity: a decision was forming in my mind. The Security Branch was beyond doubt planning an act of character assassination against me: I would not give them information out of loyalty to my friends, but they would break me finally with some carefully introduced indication that my friends had abandoned me because I had betrayed them, or so the Security Branch would arrange for the version to be told. This abandonment I would not be able to face; and even until it happened I did not have the strength to survive. There was only one way out, before I drove myself mad, and as the truest indication to anyone who was interested that I had not let the Security Branch have it all their own way. I was anguished when I thought of the children, but what good would I be to them in mental pieces? On the flyleaf of the crossword puzzle book, with the pencil that was the property of the South African Government, I wrote a note that apologized for my cowardice, loved the children once more, tried to say words that would have a special meaning for Joe, and indicated that I had not given in, that those still free should not panic and should proceed in the knowledge that I had kept

130

their secrets. After the last inspection of the night I reached for the phial of pills (which the wardress had left in the cell quite inadvertently the day two doctors had called, my own and the prison one), and swallowed the lot.

I had never thought about dying so I do not know how I expected to feel coming back into consciousness. I had no feeling at being witness to my own resurrection, only a bewildering confusion of time and place and circumstance. I thought I had moved away, but I was in the same cell. I seemed to find an easy, matter-of-fact acceptance that I had not succeeded. My mind was closed to the enormity of what I had tried to do. It might have been the same day, it might have been the one after, but suddenly the Commandant was in the cell with the wardress beside him.

'Do you want a doctor?' he asked. I nodded.

'What for? I mean what's wrong with you? Headache? Stomach ache? I have to enter something in the book.'

It was Competent's duty. 'It's her nerves,' she said shortly.

Not long after, I was afflicted by a wave of uncontrollable hysterical weeping. A prison doctor came, but I would tell him nothing and he left without discovering what anything was all about.

My weeping might have echoed through the station, or else he was snooping as usual, but then it was Viktor standing at my bedside. He took his handkerchief from his pocket and left it with me.

Days after, I assailed him for having come into the cell when I was in bed. He said, 'I had to find out what was wrong.' Some days after that he asked, 'Were you wearing a nightie or were those shortie pyjamas?'

In the daze of coming out of what seemed like a coma I remembered to rip the message from the front of the crossword puzzle book and flush it down the lavatory.

Somehow the act of taking the pills shocked away any further intention of doing so. I had completely lost track of time and even interest in keeping a wall calendar or sewing stitches behind my dressing-gown lapel; but inch by inch I made a slow adjustment to balance, though I was not sure at the time that I was doing so. I managed to have another visit from my own doctor and I told him I had taken all the pills. He was the only person I told all the while I was in prison, and I told hardly anyone when I got out. He did not seem surprised, or impressed by my surprise that the pills had not worked. 'You don't think I'd be so foolish as to leave you with that size dose?' he asked, and I could laugh about my ignorance. 'I'm heading for a crack-up, aren't I?' I asked, and he said, 'You've had one already.' He suggested that I should ask for the Government psychiatrist. But I decided that to get his intervention and convince him of the depth of my anxiety, I would have to reveal the basis for this anxiety. I was prepared to do nothing that would expose my weakness to Viktor or Klindt or any member of the Security Branch; the report of the Government psychiatrist would surely go into a file for the Branch and would be ammunition for my further destruction.

There was nothing for it but to swallow the tranquillizers which the doctor prescribed (and which I was pleased to note the wardress conscientiously kept in her office) and to try to coast back to normality. I would be on guard against a further relapse of body, of spirit, of confidence. I had sealed myself to solitary, and the longer I stayed 'inside' the more certain my friends would be that I had not capitulated. There would be security in detention!

I began to think, in as orderly a way as I could, about the methods of the Security Branch. The Minister, or police chiefs, would order an arrest. They need not announce it, in fact they seldom did. They often did not notify next-of-kin of the arrest or where the prisoner was detained. Prisoners became the un-numbered, the nameless, the scattered, the lost. Where there was no patently obvious reason for the choice of victim, like front-line battle in a trade union or mass organization, the conclusion inevitably reached was 'someone has talked' and that was the beginning of the war of nerves in which the prisoner took constant punishment.

'No Place for You'

There were the detectives with the crude approach. Van Zyl once said to me: 'You have something to sell. Sell it and get yourself out of here.' Sell others to save yourself; it was too blatant. There were the taunts: 'Your husband is a coward, on the run.' 'The leaders abroad are cowards, they are sitting drinking brandy, and leaving you to sweat in a cell.' There were the threats: 'You're too comfortable here, we'll have to find somewhere else.' Or to Africans, because brutality came as naturally as breathing when the police dealt with Africans: 'Do you know Looksmart? Unless you tell us everything, you will die in a cell like Looksmart, and your people will not know what has happened.' Flattery: 'You're an intelligent woman. You must know what we want to know and what is good for you. You have wasted your life, there is still time. . . .' Cajolery: 'Everyone's talking except you. But if you talk no one will ever know.' Official correctness: 'This is the law; we're only doing our duty.' Threats again: 'You'd be surprised at what we know. We know everything anyway.' Generosity and concern: 'You have one last chance to save yourself; if you don't talk now it will be too late.' Callousness: 'Ninety-Day detention is good for leftists.' A shifting of conscience on to the shoulders of the victim: 'We're not keeping you here. You hold the key to your release. Why are you doing this to yourself?' Tightening the screw: 'After this ninety days there will be others, and others after that. And it's no good thinking we won't know when you're lying. We know what we want from you. You have to answer questions, but to the satisfaction of the Minister, remember that.' The ominous warning: 'Everyone cracks sooner or later; we'll find your cracking point too.' Innocence: 'Interrogation under duress? Good heavens, no, not us, we've never heard of that method.' Mystery: 'Why do we want to know if we won't use the information? We have our methods, our purposes.' Importance: 'We're engaged on State business, State security; the State is behind us.'

I had always been contemptuous of the State security apparatus. The detectives were distinguishable by the tall hats and Government-issue suits they wore, by their physical appearance, I thought. Their bumbling methods brought them ridicule. But these amateurs in political sleuthing who seized books because they had 'black' or 'red' in the title had developed into sophisticated sadistic mind-breakers in the matter of a few years. The failure of the treason trial and the few frame-ups tried there had been a painful public and world humiliation. Those held in prison pending political trials or during the 1960 State of Emergency and the days of the 1961 Mandela strike, had emerged from a spell of community jail life with morale marvellously unimpaired. Every new stretch of prison for a group of political prisoners gave birth to a new batch of freedom songs. Jail spells had not broken us; they had helped to make us. The Security Branch had also been painfully aware of its failure to infiltrate informers into the movement, or get politicals themselves to change sides. Our security was good when it had not been severely tested. When solitary confinement and the torture of prolonged interrogations was introduced in the 1963 amendment to the General Laws Amendment Act, we were in for some disastrous collapses. At first I had thought the Security Branch far too unaware of human susceptibility and sensitivity to know what effect the solitary spells would have on people. Not a bit of it. We underestimated them sadly. The Security Branch had launched a deliberate plan of attack, and had studied its texts carefully. Where one detective or the other proved inept as an interrogator, the total impact of all the methods of a group of interrogators, with prolonged solitary confinement, often had its effect.

After the first score or so of detentions, the Branch began to work with some measure of confidence. The key judgement was when to apply really stiff pressure, at what moment the victim was emotionally most fragile. People's 'cracking-points' did vary; some were demoralized quite early on in their detention; others took longer; many lasted out altogether. It was so difficult to know beforehand who would fare well or badly. Men holding key positions in the political movement, who had years of hard political experience and sacrifice behind them, cracked like egg shell. Others, with quiet, reticent, self-effacing

134

natures, who had been woolly in making decisions and slow to carry them out, emerged from long spells of isolation shaken but unbroken.

Perhaps one day the South African Security Branch will plead that it used psychological torture for the benefit of science: that from its files one can study the case histories of its victims to discern 'cracking-points', resistance to suggestion, the correlation of psychological types with will and ability to exist over long periods of time in isolation. Beside longer-experienced inquisitors, the South Africans might be amateurs just beginning to learn the methods of psychological warfare; but they are learning fast. Give them time; they have the eagerness to outdo any Inquisition. Because, they tell themselves, they are only doing their duty. They all talked like little Eichmanns. There was rarely a Security Branch detective who did not say: 'It's the law, we're only doing our job.' This is the danger. Like Eichmann they will do anything in the name of their job. They will be answerable for nothing. Torture itself becomes no more than the pursuit of their daily routine.

At first torture was reserved for Africans alone. But Ninety-Day detention had not been in force for fourteen months when torture was turned against whites, even though one of the most sacred laws of apartheid had been, up to then, that whites, all whites, any whites, are different from Africans, and must be handled apart, even in the jails. With the use of torture this, too, changed. Anything was permissible to the Security Branch. The skill of the inquisitor was to know what methods to use against each prisoner. Sometimes the machine was in a hurry and there was no time to wait for the erosion that solitary confinement for a long enough period of time was almost always bound to bring about. Torture, electric shocks, beatings, were then ordered early on in the imprisonment. In other instances they were not in such a hurry or so desperate for results. The interrogators warmed to their task of studying their victims, or leaving time in solitary to make inroads on their resistance while they dealt with other cases.

I could now see unravelled the campaign of attack against

me. Solitary confinement for an undetermined period was the basic requirement. Nel would pay routine but uninterested visits, except that he would vary his introduction to each interview with a slice of good or bad news ('You have not been charged in the Rivonia trial!' or 'Your children are leaving the country!') to measure my reaction. From neglect by him I would then be introduced to the more concentrated attention of Viktor, when three months was almost up and I must be feeling the accumulated effects of so many weeks in isolation. But before he appeared with his apparent concern to spare me the worst of eventualities, I had to be subjected to carefully planted hints about a prosecution for possession of a copy of a banned magazine, which would be an enormous relief compared with the ordeal of the Rivonia trial or another spell of detention. The hints about the prosecution were carefully timed to raise my expectations of easy relief. All Viktor's talk centred round how smoothly that prosecution could be avoided. He had come to make a deal but withdrew, disappointed, when I turned the proposition down, disappointed at my stubborn refusal to save myself. Enter the villains to make the phony release and the re-arrest, but not before a visit from the children, eager and expectant for my release, had given me another emotional jar. The release and the re-arrest had come a day before the actual expiry of my ninety days, and I had lost a day and a night I might have had to adjust to their tactics of springing a surprise (the children's visit) on me before a rude shock of re-arrest. The invitation to an interrogation session had come hot-foot on the release, again before I had had time to find my balance, and on top of one shock they had not planned: the information that B. had probably given me away. I can see the instructions in The Grays' order book or wherever they keep their collection of texts: the visit of the children will elate her; surprise her by making the release a day earlier than she expects; make the release as realistic as possible; let her get out on the pavement for a whiff of the free air, pounce fast and effect the removal from the pavement to the cell as rapidly as you can, and slam that door closed yourself; pounce again the next morning when the wave of desperation has not yet receded. These tactics were not the products of any master-mind, but coming at the end of a spell of ninety days alone, in a cell, they were subtle devices. I thought I had adapted to boredom and aloneness unlimited, but inside me the effects had accumulated to obscure insight and judgement when I most needed them.

'It is still a widely held but physiologically untenable dogma,' writes Dr William Sargant in *Battle for the Mind*, 'that ill-treatment that leaves a man with a whole skin, the use of his limbs and unimpaired senses cannot be construed as duress. . . . The average man, in other words, perfectly understands physical pressure leading to breakdown but imagines that mental pressure is something that he, and therefore everyone else, is quite capable of resisting.'

'Political indoctrination,' writes J. A. C. Brown in *Techniques of Persuasion*, 'depends as much upon sympathy on the part of the inquisitor as upon threats.'

Friendliness instead of hostility. 'I'll never lose my temper with you,' Viktor told me repeatedly.

The use of a friendly period to find out everything about the detainee and win his confidence. 'I know you better after a month than people who have known you your whole life,' said Viktor.

This was after the nightmare three days of intensive scrutiny at The Grays, my shock and guilt and hysterical reaction. After he had found me in bed screaming uncontrollably Viktor stayed away for a day or so (I no longer marked the days carefully) and then he came back for regular, daily interviews. Once he forgot himself and grumbled his peeve. 'Swanepoel spoiled it all,' he said, and then stopped himself. How desperate they were for a statement and I would not give them one!

At last I permitted myself my first scent of victory. I determined to shake off the all-devouring sense of guilt at my lapse. I had been reeling towards a precipice and I had stopped myself at the edge. It had *not* been too late to beat them back. I

137

had undermined my own resistance, yet I had not after all succumbed. In the depth of my agony I *had* won.

I braced myself for continued existence in jail; if not this one, then some other. Somehow I would summon powers of survival, kill the part of me that yearned for other lives, and resign myself to continued imprisonment as the price of the life I had chosen myself. I would get used to the idea and the life in prison, and I would manage.

One morning Viktor came to ask me what I would like to read. 'What's come over you people now?' I asked. He was behaving like a smug Father Christmas. No, he said, it's just that the colonel said I could have books, one at a time, and all the titles had to be approved by Pretoria. I asked for *The Charterhouse of Parma* which I had been longing to get my hands on for over three months, and I had to give him a potted summary of the plot. He telephoned my mother who brought him a copy of the book, and the next day he brought it to me.

*

I had been re-detained for the second term on 7 November, the same day that the Minister of Justice defended the re-imposition of Ninety-Day detention on people who had completed a term without divulging anything to the police.

The following week, in the Cape Supreme Court, Mr Justice van Winsen ordered, in a court application brought on behalf of Albie Sachs, a Cape Town barrister held in detention, that Sachs be allowed a 'reasonable supply' of books and writing material. 'There can be no doubt,' said the judge, 'that the effect of solitary confinement for all but one hour of exercise a day and the deprivation of reading matter and writing material constitutes a punishment.' Two days later the Commissioner of Police told a Johannesburg newspaper that all detainees were given treatment similar to that specified in the judgement of Mr Justice van Winsen in the Sachs case. They had 'always been treated like this'. The Commissioner was 'never of the impression that the detainees had not received reasonable exercise and reading and writing material, subject, however, to the discretion of the local officer responsible

*for the detention'. He was sure that in most cases detainees had
received reading and writing material.*

*Yet the Government was lodging an appeal against the judg-
ment in the Sachs case. The Commissioner did not offer to explain
why the Government should appeal against its own standards for
detainees!*

*

I now had Stendhal and a crossword puzzle book, but Viktor
did not leave me alone. I wanted to be left to myself, yet I came
out each time he sent the wardress to fetch me. Every remark he
made inflamed my suspicions, yet I became a gullible listener
to his inconsequential talk, and even a participant. I told him I
was answering no questions and making no statement; he
undertook not to ask questions. 'Pity,' he said, 'I could learn so
much from you.' When he introduced political topics, I said that
I would not talk to him as detainee talking to a detective. When
he came for these interviews he left his working partner Van der
Merwe somewhere else. They, his fellow-detectives, knew that
he always liked to work alone, he explained. He made sure that
the door of the interview room was slightly ajar, and if it swung
to in the wind he would push it open again with his foot. He
told me about himself, how it had been a childhood ambition to
be a policeman, how his parents had wanted him to go to the
University of Stellenbosch and he had brought them papers to
sign which they thought were an entry form for the university
but which turned out to be police force enrolment forms. 'What
would you have studied at Stellenbosch?' I asked. 'Music,' he
said. He was becoming a fascinating study – even if he were
not telling the truth – but he was in a far better position to study
me than I him, and I tried to say this to myself again and again.
Often the interviews went by in a long series of jokes and
banter and chatter. He offered me cigarettes from his pack and
lit them with the lighter or matches which he kept always in the
same pocket, as he did everything he carried on his person. He
hated to see men patting their suit pockets in search of something, he said, it showed disorganization and indiscipline. I

139

called him 'Lieutenant' with the mock respect for authority in my voice, that he did not seem to hear most times. He called me 'Ruth' with the hard guttural 'r' of the Afrikaans.

I told him several times that there was no point in his coming to see me; he was wasting his time. 'I don't want to see you,' I said over and over again. 'Keep away from me.'

'Do you really mean that?' he asked. 'I've watched you when you walk out of here back to your cell, and your head drops and your shoulders slump as you go in.' He didn't think I liked it at Marshall Square. Why didn't I get myself out of the place?

He broached again the matter of a statement. I would make no statement, I repeated, because they were out to trap me. I did not trust them. 'How can we trap you on your own statement, if we don't have the evidence?' asked Viktor. 'You'll make it up if you haven't got it,' I retorted. For the first time I saw his temple throb and his hands clenched on the table between us in a fist which seemed to make a swift perhaps involuntary movement towards me. 'You've got a twisted mind,' he snarled. When his fist clenched I tilted my chin upwards in mock acceptance of the blow. He had regained control. 'I'd rather kiss it,' he said.

I loathed myself but it seemed I could not resist taking part in this exchange with another human being, talking, responding, proving I was not a caricature, a prototype, but a person. I was plagued alternately by paranoic suspicion and naïve gullibility that maybe this man *was* different from the Nels and the Swanepoels.

This is what he was trying to prove. He said as much. He could not wipe out my suspicions of the Security Branch, he said, but I should trust him. He wanted to see me out of the police station. 'This is no place for you,' he said more than once. 'You, you shut up here like a bear in a cage. It's not for you.'

*

(When Swanepoel launched his frightening, bullying verbal attack on me, Viktor had conveniently left the interrogation room. When Stephanie Kemp, the twenty-three-year-old

140

physiotherapist, had her head banged on the floor – the first white woman in South Africa to be physically assaulted by the Security Branch – Viktor was conveniently out of the room. When he returned he told Stephanie that he did not think the rough treatment had been necessary and that he would have succeeded in making her talk; in any case he would rather have had her crying on his shoulder.)

*

Viktor said repeatedly that I had to understand how the Security Branch worked. I had to convince him, my present interrogator, that I really had told the truth, the whole truth – 'And if you tell me anything it must be the truth, or I will know' – and he then personally had the power to effect my release. I laughed at that. 'You can't approve the title of a book for me to read,' I said. 'The titles have to go one by one on the telex to Pretoria for approval.' ... 'Yet you can release me.' He assured me that he could; that he had the power to make the recommendation that would open the cell door. He saw he would never get behind the wall of my hatred for the Security Branch; he was exerting every muscle to prove that he was different, susceptible to me, so that I would prove susceptible to him.

I was practising deceit but searching myself not to make it self-deception. I had to admit that I was desperate for company, to be able to talk to someone, that I was enormously relieved that it was neither the deadly deliberation of Nel nor the showy bombast of Swanepoel. Viktor came laden with calculating charm and flattery thick with treacherous intent: could I see it clearly every time he turned on the charm?

I longed to withdraw to read, but he continued to come practically every day. Once he came twice in a day. I had finished Stendhal and asked for *War and Peace*. He wanted a plot summary. As in Stendhal, I said, Napoleon figures; as an ideal in *The Charterhouse*, very much to the fore in *War and Peace*. 'What's this thing you've got about Napoleon?' he wanted to know.

He was getting to know me all the same. He sat in on a second interview with my sister-in-law; he watched a wretched tearful session with the children when the eldest sat on the ground in the exercise yard and howled her heart out with loneliness and pity for her state, and the other two were on the verge of following suit. Pretoria was still reserving judgement on *War and Peace*, but a thriller *The Night has a Thousand Eyes* came, and for the first time in my life I was afraid of a book, because the thousand eyes were the force of telepathy and I felt the eery presence of Viktor's scrutiny continually at the back of my neck.

He might have been getting impatient but he did not show it except to say his annual leave was due shortly and I should get myself out of Marshall Square before then. 'If you go on holiday leaving me here, you'll have me on your conscience, I suppose?' I said. His job as a policeman was very important to him. He was filled with ambition for promotion, anxious to study law in his spare time to qualify sooner and better. I sneered at the study of criminology which I guessed policemen undertake. He agreed there was not much in the theory of criminal types. He believed above all that a policeman needed to watch human behaviour, and that in action, in the course of detection and talking to prisoners about their associates in crime, he came to know them. He sometimes saw his victims in jail and he prided himself that none of them nursed a grievance against him; he treated them fairly and played the game, and they realized the game was up when he had caught them. That was his version of himself as detective.

It seemed that this would go on for ever. I had read only three books in a fortnight and still Viktor came to the little interview room and we conducted verbal activity, screened and filtered by him and by me, but human contact nevertheless. I was no longer so affected by the gloom of the cell; my own state was not of despair as much as resignation. I had had worse days than these.

He came on a Saturday morning to press me again to get

myself out of detention. We talked, but of nothing. He came back that afternoon to make the same suggestion. I remarked that it was Robyn's birthday party the following day, Sunday, and he said, 'I know. I wasn't going to mention it because I didn't want to upset you, but now that you've raised it I want to tell you that I can get you home for the party. Would you like to go?'

Of course not, I said. Fancy being paraded home for a children's party and then being escorted back to prison. I wouldn't dream of it.

No, he said, I had misunderstood him. He didn't mean going to the party on parole, but that he would arrange for my complete release in time for the party – if I made a statement in time. He would be going home immediately after leaving Marshall Square and would be available any time of Saturday night or Sunday morning. If need be he would work through the night for me. Everyone at Marshall Square knew his telephone number and I had only to ask for a telephone call to be made to him: he would be instantly at my service.

I spent a wretched week-end. I entertained no notion of calling Viktor to buy a release, but I had an attack of gloom at being locked up and especially during the birthday week-end. The Sunday dragged interminably.

The following morning I was still washing in the bucket of hot water when the wardress came to tell me that Viktor was waiting.

I was so polite. 'I kept you waiting?' I asked.

'I've come to take you home,' he said. 'I've got an order for your release.'

'Look here,' I said. 'Don't try *that* again. You've done it to me once already, and it's cruel. I won't have it done again.'

'Honestly, I have an order for your release. Van der Merwe is in the charge office fixing it up. You can get ready to leave.'

I burst into tears. I continued to sit in that interview room for several hours. I did not believe the release was genuine. 'You're going to re-arrest me?' 'No.' 'Prosecute me?' 'No.'

After all that I was not even prosecuted for possession of the illegal magazine.

I don't know why I was released. Perhaps they just didn't have enough evidence. Perhaps they had made up their minds that I would not talk after all. Perhaps I was approaching another cracking-point, a cracking not wide open to them, but of myself, and they might have seen it coming. Viktor said he knew me by then better than I knew myself.

My release had to be part of a wider tactic for dealing with political whites, the errants who would not go into the *laager* of whites against Africans. How deal with us? Some were permitted to leave the country: this was one way of physically removing opposition. If among those locked up there were men who broke under the strain of detention and interrogation, they would be used for information by the Security Branch. Those who were unbreakable were given long spells of imprisonment – eight years, twelve years, twenty years, life. In my case the first spell of detention had not given them the information they wanted from me, nor the evidence in all its strength that they needed to convict me. They could have been releasing me to watch me again and catch me in the act. Viktor delivered a warning against my trying to evade my bans or make a dash over the border by the escape route. 'If you try that,' he said, 'I'll be there to catch you.'

We left Marshall Square eventually and by the time I got home it was lunch-time, though Viktor had brought his release order early that morning. When they left me in my own house at last I was convinced that it was not the end, that they would come again.